SOCIALLY AWARE

MAKING IT THROUGH THE DAY
WITH A SMILE

FRANK SORGE

Frank Sorge/Socially Aware
Printed in the United States of America

Socially Aware/ Frank Sorge -- 1st ed.

ISBN 9798585940873 Print Edition

CONTENTS

This book is dedicated to my Mother.
Her continuing guidance, love, and support has shaped me into the person I am. Anything I accomplish in life is only a reflection of her.

CHAPTER 1

THE GREAT SHIFT IN THE HUMAN CONDITION

———

"So many of us are reaching out, hoping someone out there will grab our hands and remind us that we are not as alone as we fear." –Roxane Gay

———

Modern society hums at the breakneck speed of electronic connections. Our texts, instant messages, and social media posts whizz through cyberspace. Did you know that eight trillion text messages are sent every day worldwide? That's 15.2 million text messages per minute! On average, Americans send and receive about ninety-four text messages per day. That's a whirlwind of reading, typing or dictating, and sending. With all the chatter, surely people are feeling more connected than ever—right?

Almost everything can be ordered for next-day delivery with the touch of a button. More of us are working remotely, ordering food delivery, binge-watching our favorite shows, and playing games on our phones and tablets. We have fewer serendipitous encounters in which we connect with friends, acquaintances, even strangers. We used to talk on the phone to conduct personal business, but now if we call a medical office or a cable company, for example, we're stuck in an endless loop of automated systems that gather our information.

Virtual existence is convenient, fast, and furious, but is it good for us?

Experts are sounding the alarm about a loneliness crisis in America. It's hardly comforting to think we're not alone in our loneliness. Loneliness in the U.S. is an epidemic like the opioid crisis—and, although less deadly, it can harm our physical and mental health. The average American has only one close friend, and a surprising one in four people have no confidantes at all. According to *Cigna's U.S. Loneliness Index*, a survey of more than 20,000 American adults ages 18 and older, nearly half of Americans said they sometimes or always feel alone or left out. One in four Americans rarely feel understood, and one in five people report feeling close to people seldom or never.

What Has Changed?

Have Americans always been this lonely, or has something changed in American society? Over the past fifty years, the number of U.S. households composed of one person has more than doubled. Single-person households are now one of the most common household types, even more common than married couples with children. Over a quarter of the U.S. population—and 28 percent of older adults—live alone. This solitude is most common in urban areas, where around 40 percent of households have single occupants. In some areas of Manhattan and Washington, D.C., it is as high as 65 percent.

Americans aren't as active in civic institutions, churches, community groups, clubs, teams, and volunteer organizations as they were for hundreds of years. These institutions have always provided safety nets, meeting places, mentoring, and meaning and purpose. Also, older cherished traditions that have stood the test of time, like gathering for a meal with family and friends, have become less common. Without a substitute for community support, people are flying solo, often searching for what's missing in their lives.

In *Alienated America*, Tim Carney tackles issues of alienation and loneliness. He maintains that the real source of isolation comes from the erosion of institutions in America, including religion, marriage, and community. He says alienation happens when people lack these institutions to connect with others. Alienation is a state of mind that's not just being distant from society but not even seeing the purpose of society. Rootless men, whose lives are bereft of meaning, may be contributing to the mass shooting events in America.

Who's Lonely?

If I were to tell you that it's not older people but the younger generations who are the loneliest, would you be surprised? Gen Z (ages 18-22) had the highest loneliness scores, trailed by millennials (ages 23-37). The Greatest Generation (ages 72+) were the least lonely. More than half of Gen Zers feel left out or isolated from others and identify with the feelings associated with loneliness. In contrast, only a quarter of people 72 or older feel left out or isolated from others.

Baby boomers are aging alone more than any generation in our nation's history. Unlike their parents, baby boomers typically had fewer children, and their marriages were more likely to have ended in divorce than previous generations. In fact, more than a quarter of baby boomers are either divorced or were never married. As a result, roughly one in six baby boomers now lives alone.

Loneliness afflicts millennials as well, and the prospect of even greater loneliness haunts them. Loneliness is the number one fear of young people today—ranking ahead of losing a home or a job. In fact, 42 percent of millennial women are more afraid of loneliness than of being diagnosed with cancer. The fear of missing out (FOMO) stems from the feeling that life is going on without them. FOMO is defined as the blend of anxiety, inadequacy, and irritation that can flare up while skimming social media.

We have so many ways to connect with each other—calling, texting, instant messaging, Facetiming, Snapchatting, and chatting on social media. What has gone wrong? Is it a lack of face-to-face opportunities for people to connect in meaningful ways?

In her *Forbes* article, "Why Millennials Are Lonely," author Caroline Beaton writes, "The internet temporarily enhances the social satisfaction and behavior of lonely people, who are more likely to go online when they feel isolated, depressed, or anxious." Taken alone, the use of social media is not a predictor of loneliness. But it's interesting to note that older generations, who have lower loneliness scores, are less inclined to use social media than younger generations.

The Hazards of Loneliness

Did you know that loneliness and social isolation can be as damaging to health as smoking fifteen cigarettes or drinking more than six alcoholic drinks a day? Loneliness is even worse for longevity than being obese or physically inactive. The lack of connection can be life-threatening; seclusion has been associated with cardiovascular problems and premature death. Loneliness can impact workplace productivity; lonely individuals are often less satisfied with their jobs and are more often unemployed. It is commonly correlated with mental health issues such as anxiety, depression, and suicidal tendencies.

Living alone, being unmarried (single, divorced, widowed), no participation in social groups, fewer friends, and strained relationships are risk factors not only for increased loneliness but also for premature mortality. Retirement and physical impairments may also increase the risk of social isolation.

Few aspects of community are more potent than the degree of connectedness and social support. "We view a person's physical, mental, and social health as being connected," said David M. Cordani, president and chief executive officer of Cigna. "It's for this reason that we regularly examine the physical, mental, and social needs of our people and the communities they live in. In analyzing this closely, we're seeing a lack of human connection, which ultimately leads to a lack of vitality—or a disconnect between mind and body. We must change this trend by reframing the conversation to be about 'mental wellness' and 'vitality' to speak to our mental-physical connection. When the mind and body are treated as one, we see powerful results."

Human beings are hardwired to be social creatures; our nervous systems settle with others around us. Biology, neuroscience, and psychology indicate our bodies tend to work better when we're in the company of others. Perhaps it is the sense that we are stronger in numbers; our survival has always depended upon our interconnectedness.

Simulating Social Interaction

Many people who lack connection in their lives turn to the digital realm to allay their feelings of isolation. Unfortunately, thousands of followers and hundreds of likes are not the cure for loneliness. Research shows that loneliness is caused by a lack of depth in relationships. The risk with collaborative technology is that it simulates social interaction rather than offering meaningful connections. This false sense of connectedness can lead you to believe you have less need for real-life social connections.

A survey looking at the social media patterns of nearly 2,000 young adults found that people who logged in for thirty minutes a day were less lonely than those who logged into social media for more than two hours. Participants who logged in nine times per week felt less isolated than those who checked social media over fifty times a week. In other words, more is not necessarily better. But it's important to note that the use of social media did not predict loneliness. The critical factor is how social media is used. Thus, a strategic and well-thought-out approach to social media use is likely to result in greater overall satisfaction with modern life.

Drowning in a Sea of Information

To have so much information at our fingertips is like having a magical genie granting our every wish. But it has created another problem unique to the internet age: information overload. By one calculation, we've produced more information in the last ten years than in all human history before that. This is more information than the brain is configured to handle, or at the very least, more than it has ever handled before. The conscious mind can pay attention to three, maybe four, things at once. If you exceed that, you begin to exercise poorer judgment, you lose track of things, and you lose your focus.

For a decade, University of Nevada, Las Vegas sociologist Simon Gottschalk studied the social and psychological effects of new information and communication technologies. According to Gottschalk, "Our devices constantly expose us to a barrage of colliding and clamoring messages." The unending stream of alerts and pings "deteriorates how we approach our everyday activities, deforms how we relate to each other, and erodes a stable sense of self. It leads to burnout at one end of the continuum and to depression at the other."

Think about it: each time we're notified of alerts, breaking news, texts, and emails on our smartphone, we feel compelled to check. But compulsively checking our phones interrupts the flow of life. Like a technological narcissist, the smartphone demands our attention, and we grant it. Because you never know: the next notification could be life-changing—right? It usually isn't, but the allure of an incoming message pulls us into the world of our smartphone and away from what's happening around us in the real world.

Digital Vitriol

Not only are we drowning in a sea of information, we often encounter digital vitriol when we post our opinions on discussion boards or in social media forums. People can even be ostracized for speaking their point of view or deterred from voicing their opinion to begin with. This happens more commonly with political, religious, and other controversial topics.

If you've spent any time reading blogs or articles online, you've noticed that online interactions aren't always civilized; in fact, they can quickly turn nasty. An internet article that posits a given position spurs hundreds of comments, some of which are people railing against the author and each other. Soon, the exchanges devolve into personal attacks and obscenities. Why are we so mean behind our screens? One study finds many of us harbor an inner troll. What is a troll? It is a person who initiates arguments or upsets people on the internet to sow discord by posting inflammatory messages in an online community with the intent of provoking readers, whether for the troll's amusement or a specific gain.

When you read a personal attack from a troll and you're vulnerable, you're more likely to mimic the troll's behavior. There's no eye contact or body language to read, so it's harder to see the humanity in people and easier to objectify and classify them. Bottom line: We tend to be mean from behind our screens because there are no immediate repercussions.

We should respect everyone's rights to speak their mind, no matter our personal differences. Differences of opinion and being malicious are completely different things. We need to respect all people's right to their opinions and be secure enough with our own beliefs that we aren't threatened when someone disagrees. This is called healthy debate, and it seems to be a lost art form in this age of division and partisan politics.

Automation Anxiety

Another trend changing the landscape of society is workplace automation. Technology is moving toward making many types of human labor obsolete. Around 25 percent of jobs in the U.S. are at "high risk" of automation because 70 percent or more of their tasks could be done by machines. Another 36 percent of jobs are at "medium risk" as a machine could do between 30 and 70 percent of their tasks. Some 40 percent of jobs are at "low risk," with less than 30 percent of their tasks able to be performed by a robot. What will people do when technology takes over so many jobs? That's a huge insecurity in the back of Americans' minds. They're insecure about their worth and viability in the new world order.

In fact, automation and robotics may be causing anxiety in workers over job security—leading to poorer health. At one time it was assumed that robots would primarily replace assembly jobs in factories, but now software systems threaten managerial and other professional jobs.

On some level, innovation is rendering us more useless; almost every technological advancement can be argued as creating a more efficient version of the species. From an economic standpoint, technological innovations from the wheel to the iPhone have made us more efficient in the short term but obsolete in the long-term economic cycle.

At the end of the day, we're an anxious bunch, addicted to our phones, tablets, and computers and worried about our job security—forces that drive alienation and loneliness. It is high time we evaluated the technological tools at our disposal to enhance and not usurp our lives. We should be the masters and not the other way around. If the way we're using technology and social media is making us miserable and even unwell in some cases, we must change the way we're living our lives. If thinking about de-prioritizing your digital devices fills you with dread and anxiety, it's probably the very thing you must consider.

CHAPTER 2

SOCIAL MEDIA:
THE GREAT SOCIAL EXPERIMENT

Imagine that you're visiting Earth for the first time with no prior knowledge of the planet or its inhabitants and you see Earthlings' eyes fixated on rectangular lights in their hands. Wherever they go, whatever they do, even while interacting with fellow Earthlings, they gaze at the lighted gadgets. You might assume that these illuminated devices are the true overlords. You learn that Earth's inhabitants are communicating, connecting, and consuming via these tools. But it seems that they're entranced and under a spell.

Often when there's a culture shift and new technology or ways of doing things are introduced, it takes time for human development to catch up. Such is the case with social media, the internet, and smartphones. The internet went mainstream in 1993. And social media was first adopted in 2003 with the advent of Myspace. Smartphones were first introduced in 1992 but didn't become mainstream until the early 2010s. In the grand scheme of things, twenty-seven years, sixteen years, and nine years are inconsequential. But in that period, we've virtually restructured how we do almost everything—living, dating, relating, working, shopping, researching, gathering, sharing information, and expressing our opinions. In short, almost nothing is untouched. And as with so many new societal and cultural developments, humans with access to these tools jumped on the bandwagon and never looked back. But an evaluation is in order. Why? Because psychologists are sounding the alarm about its effects.

—————

"The most powerful tech companies in the world are making deliberate decisions that do great harm."
–Tristan Harris, former Google employee

—————

The Downsides of Social Media

Social media is as addictive as cigarettes, but social media isn't sanctioned like tobacco. What makes social media any different? Your brain releases dopamine every time you see a picture or get a like, so you're going back for more, and you get legitimately chemically addicted. For some, besides being addictive, social media is associated with psychological problems like anxiety, depression, and loneliness. Because people typically access social media using smartphones, their usage is intertwined and contributes to excessive checking, typically stemming from FOMO.

Even if social media use didn't cause psychological problems, many people's social media use is habitual. This usage can affect other areas of their lives and can even be dangerous, such as checking smartphones while driving. Other behaviors may be irritating or impolite, such as accessing social media while dining out with friends or checking your smartphone while watching a movie at the theater. Snubbing social contact with friends or preferring to engage with social media on your smartphone instead of being fully present is called "phubbing."

Comparison Depression

Social media can trigger sadness and a decreased sense of well-being. We tend to compare ourselves to others on Facebook, Instagram, LinkedIn, Twitter, and Snapchat. It's a natural human instinct to judge our success in life by seeing how we measure up. We have always looked to others to measure our progress in life. The only thing that's different now is this tendency is playing out on our digital devices. Studies show that comparing ourselves with others on social media makes us depressed. And, let's face it, because people typically post the good stuff, we're comparing ourselves to an illusion of fulfillment and accomplishment.

Highlight Reel of Life

When you look at your friends' Instagram and Facebook pages, you're not likely to see many makeup-less photos in which people who look like crap are slouching on the couch, bingeing on potato chips. You're going to see the highlight reel of their life. Where did they go on vacation? What upscale restaurant did they go to? What fancy dish did they enjoy? Who were they with that was famous or notable? How many best friends do they do fun things with—like ziplining, bungee jumping, rafting, and ballooning? Based on their posts, they're living their best lives, having the time of their lives, always having peak moments, and marking things off their bucket lists. In fact, it seems that their life is a series of bucket-list items.

People typically post a highlight reel of their life, creating an iceberg illusion; people post their best moments. What you don't see is the massive iceberg under the water—the hard work, the day in and day out grind, the unsexy moments, the intense focus and drive that it takes to achieve anything in life. People don't see the whole iceberg; they just see the tip of the iceberg that looks so nice and wonderful. Or even worse, they are so concerned with making themselves appear successful that they never live up to their full potential. For example, one of your friends might have worked hard for years, and he finally got the chance to take a vacation to the Amalfi Coast in Italy. He posted photos of himself next to a dramatic coastline plunging into the Mediterranean Sea because he was so darned proud of himself, and he deserved it. But you're sitting on the couch thinking, *I must be a loser. He's having the time of his life while I'm here in my sweatpants binge-watching* The Sopranos.

Everyone pulls the highlight reel of their life because they want to share the good times, but if everyone is sharing the good times, no one sees the bad, and everyone wonders if they're the only one having the bad times. Everyone does have bad times, but this skewed focus triggers a chain reaction of negative thinking.

Social Media Is a Fake Existence

Let's face it: Social media is a fake existence. The truth is, life is messy; relationships are challenging; work is, well, hard work; and things don't always go the way you planned. It's good to keep these things in mind as you scroll through dozens of posts or check out someone's perfect-looking social media page. The girl who's posing in front of a waterfall (woo-hoo!) with the perfect body and the

I-love-life expression may have just had a fight with her boyfriend right before the pic was taken. If you keep that in mind—that social media is basically a fake existence—you'll be less bothered as you engage with your favorite social media sites.

Nature of Friendships

More friends on social media doesn't mean you're more social. Just because you're popular on Facebook doesn't mean you have more friends than anyone else, according to a recent study. The research found online friends were not the same as real-world friends, and social media doesn't let you expand your friendship circle beyond traditional limits.

Platform of Delusions

Some people think once they get a social media platform, they'll go viral, attract a huge fanbase, monetize their site or channel, and become rich and famous. Although a select group of lucky people have done this, most people out there won't achieve fame and fortune, and especially not through social media. The truth is: No matter what you do, a small group of people are going to be the best at it, and there will always be somebody better. Even if you are the best today, tomorrow someone will surpass you. Adding social media to the equation might boost your business or career, but fame and fortune are longshots.

Everyone has a platform. People confuse someone having a platform with actual value. Some people with tens of thousands of followers on social media are absolute idiots. They spew nonsense and people listen. Because if someone has so many followers, they must be offering valuable and life-changing information—right?

Living to Post

There have been instances of people updating their Facebook and Twitter accounts from the altar while getting married. Yes, really. This is a viable way to document your life, but it can also become a burden that takes you out of the moment. If you're living through the lens of social media instead of directly interacting with it, your experiences are going to be compromised and will be less memorable.

Checking, Endless Checking

Tech designers have turned so many of us into people with obsessive-compulsive disorder (OCD). OCD is characterized by unreasonable thoughts and fears (obsessions) that lead to compulsive behaviors. Before you say—not me—consider that millennials check their phones 150 times a day on average. And even if you're not a millennial, the other demographics aren't far behind. Checking, checking, always checking. What are we checking for? Updates, posts, likes, comments, friend requests—most of which aren't life-changing but supply periodic dopamine hits to our addicted brains.

Reputation Destruction

It's highly divisive and dangerous to denigrate a group of people without evidence, to slander someone and ruin their reputation without proving they've even done the thing they've been accused of. It's tragic to see wonderful people get taken down at the kneecaps after one bad thing that may or may not be true. For example, a Rochester, New York, news anchor misspoke when he said, "Martin Luther Coon" and then corrected himself by saying, "King" immediately after. Clearly, he just misspoke. You could tell he just wanted to kill himself right there. He sincerely apologized right on camera but was fired from his job anyway.

Think about it, a man who speaks for a living made a speaking error and was fired for it. Mistakes and acts of hostility or aggression are completely different things, but we've blurred the lines in a way that is truly dangerous.

Social Media Intimidation

Although it is beneficial for people to learn new information and evolve, social media intimidation is hypocritical and dangerous. The groups of people who are supposedly caring for the voices of everyone may be responsible for many people not being able to speak their minds. Most things are grey, not black and white. Some make grey issues black and white and then try people in the court of public opinion. To intimidate people from speaking their beliefs and point of view, no matter what those are, is wrong. All people should be able to speak their mind. It is up to each of us to sort through the noise and develop our own beliefs and point of view based on fact.

The Upsides of Social Media

If used judiciously, social media can be a powerful tool for connecting with like-minded people and keeping in touch with contacts. For example, Tweetups are in-person get-togethers prompted by Twitter connections, meetings that would not have happened without social media. Social media can connect people in a profound way. That was one of its intended purposes. It's a healthy social media experience to share ideas with like-minded individuals in a positive light. Groups of people get a chance to bond from different walks of life and places that might never meet offline in a million years, which is awesome. But if you're able to communicate with them face-to-face or even through phone calls, you should be doing that. Get people's phone numbers and become a part of their life; take it a step further than just connecting in this group. Form relationships, and don't keep them at arm's length.

Social media can also be a great virtual watercooler. With remote work on the rise, how do remote workers stay connected to people in their home offices? They take breaks and connect with friends and colleagues on social media. That way, they don't feel so cut off from humanity while cranking out work and meeting deadlines at home.

Social media can be a great form of sports and news consumption. For anything from financial articles to sports scores and highlights, Twitter can be a great way to sort through news while not wasting an hour or more watching the show/game/recap on television.

Social media can be a form of information distillation. For example, let's say you're planning a vacation, and you have gathered tips from friends posting travel pics and advice. You can use the curated information from trusted sources and people who share your values and sensibilities to plan your trip.

Crowdsourcing is another effective use of social media. Let's say you are writing a book and your book designer has given you three book cover options. You know which book cover you prefer, but you want to determine which cover appeals to the most people. Crowdsourcing on social media is a quick and easy way to gather information from friends and acquaintances. You post the three covers and ask for people to vote and comment. Quickly you discover that the crowd prefers a different cover. Had you not crowdsourced your cover, you'd never have known which one had the widest appeal.

The Truth About Our Social Media Consumption

How would you feel if I told you that you would spend five years and four months of your life on social media? According to a survey, internet users now spend an average of two hours and twenty-two minutes per day on social networking and messaging platforms. The total time spent on social media beats time spent eating and drinking, socializing, and grooming! American adults spend more than eleven hours a day watching, reading, listening to, or simply interacting with media, according to a study by market-research group Nielsen.

Broken down, time spent on social media differs across each platform. YouTube ranks first, consuming, on average, over forty minutes of a person's day. Facebook users spend thirty-five minutes a day. Snapchat and Instagram follow with twenty-five minutes and fifteen minutes spent per day, respectively. Finally, users will spend approximately one minute on Twitter.

What could you do over your lifetime instead? Fly to the moon and back thirty-two times, climb Mt. Everest thirty-two times, or run over 10,000 marathons. Or, instead of planning your lunar, high alpine, and endurance sport adventures, you might think about the things you could do that will get you closer to your dreams. If your goal is to become a social media guru, by all means continue honing your social media prowess. But if not, it's best to structure your day with your dreams and goals in mind. Later in this book, I will give you tools and strategies for doing just that.

All is not lost in the world of social media. There is some good news. Studies indicate there may be a sweet spot when it comes to the amount of time you spend on social media. Keeping your use down to just thirty minutes a day can lead to better mental health outcomes, according to research published in the *Journal of Social and Clinical Psychology*. When study volunteers cut down their social media use to thirty minutes per day total, they experienced a significant improvement in well-being, exhibiting reduced loneliness and depression. And anxiety and FOMO decreased as well.

How Is Social Media Affecting You?

Now for the moment of truth. It's time to find out if social media is negatively affecting you. Take this survey and answer as honestly as possible. Then add up the points based on the number values next to your corresponding answer choices. Ready to begin?

How much time do you spend on social media per day?
1. 1 hour or less
2. 2-3 hours
3. 4-5 hours

How dependent are you on your phone/tablet?
1. I can go days without it.
2. I can go many hours without it.
3. I can't even go an hour without it.

Do you feel compelled to share most of your life experiences on social media?
1. No
2. Sometimes
3. Yes

If you knew you couldn't share an experience on social media, would you pursue the experience anyway?

1. Yes
2. Maybe
3. No

Does the number of likes you receive on social media affect how you feel about yourself?

1. No
2. Sometimes
3. Yes

Do you frequently feel jealous of other people's lives on social media?

1. No
2. Sometimes
3. Yes

When scrolling through friends' posts on social media, does it make you depressed?

1. Never
2. Sometimes
3. Quite often

Does social media interfere with your in-person interactions with people?

1. Never
2. Sometimes
3. Quite often

Do you feel that social media has enhanced your life?

1. Yes
2. Sometimes
3. No

Now add up your points. If the total is between 21 and 27, social media is negatively affecting you. If your total is between 14 and 20, social media is having a somewhat negative effect. And if your total is between 9 and 13, social media is not affecting you negatively; in fact, it may be positively influencing your life.

Your Survey Results in Action

You can tweak your social media use simply by looking at your survey results. What aspects of social media are causing you anxiety or depression? Which aspects are negatively affecting your self-esteem? If, for example, the number of likes you receive affects how you feel about yourself, rethink that aspect of social media. Uncouple "likes" from your self-worth; they are not an indication of your value. They are simply someone else's subjective evaluation. As the old saying goes, "What others think about you is none of your business." I know it's easier said than done to stop living for likes, but perhaps try for a week to detach by not even looking at your likes. Then, if you notice you feel better, make it a habit to unplug from likes altogether.

If scrolling through friends' posts depresses you, don't depend on the social media company's algorithms to prioritize posts for you; instead, structure your social media activity yourself. Perhaps just visit your friends' pages or accounts to see what's new. Then jump off as soon as you've seen what they're up to.

If you feel that life isn't worth experiencing without posting on social media, try an experiment. Plan something fun, festive, or adventurous, and by all means, take photos, but know that you won't post a single pic to social media. Reflect on your experience after the fact. Was your experience any less fun? Was it, in fact, more fun without the self-consciousness that comes from the pressure to pose for posts?

You get the picture—pun intended! Take your survey results and identify the aspects causing you grief. Limit or eliminate those things, and I guarantee that you'll still have a healthy and happy existence. You get to pick and choose how to make social media work best for you!

Consider Going on a Social Media Fast

You may want to consider a social media fast, especially if you found by taking the survey that social media is negatively affecting you. What will a fast do for you? A social media fast allows you to center and rediscover your passions, values, and relationships without looking through the prism of likes and shares. It will turn off the external noise and allow you to hear your internal voice—that which guides you and helps you make the best life choices. It will also allow you to become more focused, productive, and less scatterbrained.

Now, be aware that because social media is designed to be addictive, when you first stop using it, you can expect to feel withdrawal symptoms. Researchers claim this is due to the naturally ingrained fear of missing out. But the withdrawal symptoms will be temporary. What's on the other side of the withdrawal is well worth any pain and discomfort you may feel.

Social media fasts can include taking a break for a day, a week, or even a month! If you do a more intensive fast, you will want to have other hobbies and activities lined up to fill the void. Another approach is deleting social media apps from your phone, so you can only access those sites from your computer. That way, you remove much of the temptation.

Fasts can also include simple steps, such as turning off sound notifications and allowing yourself to check your smartphone just once an hour. Other approaches include allotting times during the day for self-imposed non-screen time and leaving your smartphone in a separate room from where you sleep (thus removing the ability to check social media before bedtime, during the night, and when you wake up).

The bottom line is, only you and your friends and family know if social media is compromising your happiness and quality of life. Social media is just a tool that we have at our disposal to enhance life. You should call the shots and not the other way around. If you suspect after reading this chapter and taking the survey that social media is not serving you, rethink how you engage with it and use it to live your best possible life—leaving a smile on your face and, at the end of the day, having provided for yourself and the people you love.

CHAPTER 3

VICTIMHOOD AS CURRENCY

"Discontent, blaming, complaining, and self-pity cannot serve as a foundation for a good future, no matter how much effort you make." –Eckhart Tolle

Lately in America, it seems that victimhood is something to aspire to, as if the more you've been victimized, the higher your status in society. Some Americans are locked in competition for who is the most victimized. And in making the case for the greatest victim, they believe they are entitled to certain privileges. Some of those crying "victim" believe they deserve to be elevated to a status that is morally superior to the perceived victimizing forces. In other words, they are using victimhood as a type of currency to buy their way into a special class of people who have been wronged and deserve special dispensation. It's important to point out that this position is not limited to one political group; those on the right, left, or in the center are all guilty. It stems not just from a few select cultural or societal groups; members from every group are guilty of a victimhood mentality.

Sociologists Bradley Campbell and Jason Manning argue that the U.S. is transitioning to a victimhood culture in which people are encouraged to think of themselves as weak, marginalized, and oppressed. As if, somewhere along the way, it became the cool thing to do.

The best example I can give is to consider moving forward after the death of someone you deeply care about. After a death such as this, you will get perhaps the greatest amount of undivided attention you will ever get in your whole life. More than your birthday, more than your wedding day, and more than every family holiday you have ever been part of. And even then, amidst the most profound pain you have ever felt, 99 percent of people will have gone back to their daily lives within a month. Why? Was it out of some malicious intent? Do you have a weak support system? No, it's because the world keeps on spinning, the clock keeps on ticking, and it will never stop for any of us. And if it only stops for a few weeks for the death of a loved one, how long do you really think it should stop because someone called you a mean name or said something about you that wasn't true?

If you have never experienced this, trust that I am right, and the weeks of attention are fleeting, and the only person who will help you feel better is you. Above all else, continue to show those most important to you that they are, in fact, the most important people in your life. Because time flies, and you never know what tomorrow brings.

What is a culture of victimhood? A culture of victimhood is characterized by concern with status and sensitivity to slight with a heavy reliance on intervening parties. People can't tolerate affronts—even if unintentional—and so they report insults to authorities or broadcast them on social media. Victimization seeks pity, so rather than tapping into inner strength and demonstrating self-confidence, the victimized showcase their persecution.

Within that culture of victimhood, individuals suffer from a mentality or a mindset which feels persecuted to gain attention or avoid responsibility. People who feel like victims believe that life is not only out of their control but is out to get them. This belief results in blame fueled by self-righteous disdain. In short, having a victim mentality means that you blame other people and circumstances for your unhappiness.

If you think about it, when people make a huge case every time they feel they've been wronged, it is like children complaining every time they don't get their way. So, in a way, some Americans sound like whiny children tattling whenever things don't go their way.

How did this happen? We were once a nation of rugged, innovative, courageous self-starters who believed in our ability to carve out the American dream. Could you imagine early settlers or even beleaguered immigrants escaping religious and other persecution playing the victim because they didn't get their way? By definition, they were men and women of action, ingenuity, and initiative. The grumbling and passivity that characterizes victimhood would have been counterproductive and, in some cases, fatal.

Now, whether there are forces beyond your control making things "fair" or "unfair" is beside the fact. By far, the most important thing to understand is that no one has ever achieved mediocrity, much less success, by worrying about semantics such as these. Fair and unfair is like black and white; it's all an illusion. Most situations can be viewed as fair or unfair, depending on the way you frame them. Although this statement may sound harsh, everyone is responsible for playing the best hand with the cards they've been dealt. Whatever advantage or disadvantage you have, it is up to each individual person to be their own role model and carve out the life they desire.

"Life is not fair, it never was, and it isn't now, and it won't ever be. Do not fall into the entitlement trap of feeling like you're a victim. You are not." – **Matthew McConaughey**

How does a culture of victimhood play out? People manufacture hardship so they can claim victimhood status. Some kids from middle, upper-middle, and upper-class families pretend they have it harder than they do. They want to feel special and unique, and they do it through victimhood and manufacturing hardships instead of going out and making a difference in the world. These victim-y types think everyone is supposed to care because they've been wronged. But what they don't realize is that everyone is wronged every day. In fact, someone is being wronged every second of every day. And being wronged doesn't make them special; it just makes them human.

People must understand that just because somebody wronged them, it does not mean they have a compelling platform. Yet social media has created a culture where everyone feels their opinion matters. In fact, narcissism flourishes in today's environment. Narcissism is the pursuit of gratification from vanity or egoistic admiration of one's idealized self-image and attributes. The internet's easy access to the world stage gives people the false impression that they matter more than they do. The truth is, the world cares very little about most people's points of view or the ways they may have been wronged.

It's easy to manufacture something that garners attention that is not in your best interest. This is common with people who dwell on the negative. People are programmed to be more negative than positive. For example, on Yelp, how many positive restaurant reviews do you see versus negative? Look at the ratio. It's common to remember negative experiences more than positive experiences. They stick out in your mind. Human survival depends on being hypervigilant to threats and other negative experiences, so it's likely a hardwired tendency. But positive things happen throughout the day, and you probably don't take the time to appreciate them.

The Roots of Victimhood

How did we get here—to the place where victims are heralded as heroes? For many young adults, their preciousness begins in childhood. So-called helicopter parents hover over their children and intervene whenever there's a hurdle or a problem. And while their intentions are good, their children have less practice coping with difficulties and handling conflicts on their own, which is a critical part of becoming an independent adult.

According to psychologist Dr. Russell Thackeray, "It appears the current generation of people lacking the skill sets to have structure and discipline, without the strategies to combat personal entitlement, and without the toolkits to fail and learn, may be about to unleash a generation of victims into the world."

Victimhood Culture Is Bad for Society

Does it matter that we've become a culture of victimhood? Yes, very much so. Victimhood makes it difficult, if not impossible, for us to resolve political and social conflicts. The culture promotes a mentality that eliminates healthy discourse—turning every difference of opinion into a battle between us (good) and them (bad).

In politics and religion, it's easy to get pigeonholed—to become entrenched in your views. You're either going to extremely agree or disagree with the person you're talking to, and that approach won't lead to a productive conversation. If you're going to extremely agree with somebody, you won't get to the bottom of anything. You'll pat yourself on the back and talk about how you guys are right. On the other hand, if you extremely disagree, unless you're with a highly emotionally intelligent individual, you're less likely to find a solution to the problem. You're just going to hear the other person out and grow further attached to your position.

In 2010, social psychologists from Stanford University conducted three experiments demonstrating that feeling wronged leads to a sense of entitlement and to self-centered behavior. Their conclusion: victimhood culture makes for worse citizens—people who are less helpful, more entitled, and more selfish.

A Victim Mentality Is Bad for You

How does embracing a victim mentality affect you personally? There are perks, which can keep some victim-y types hooked. People can become addicted to playing the victim. Face it: We've all seen people who milk victimhood. In fact, it is the foundation of their identity. So, what are the perks of playing the victim?

- You feel special because you feel that you have suffered more than most people.
- You expect to be compensated/rewarded for your suffering.
- Other people will cater to you because you've been through so much.
- You're the center of attention when you air your struggles and drama.
- You don't have to take responsibility because you've earned suffering credits.
- You wait for others to give you your much-deserved benefits.

By playing the victim, you might receive temporary strokes, sympathy, and other perks, but perpetuating a victimhood identity is not in your long-term self-interest. While you might feel emboldened in your victimhood and look for justification from societal forces, this mentality will keep you stuck. Why? Because you are relinquishing your power to external forces, admitting that your only recourse is to resign yourself to the cards that life deals you instead of going out and initiating personal, professional, and societal change. While there's merit in identifying and acknowledging forces that discriminate against or oppress a group you're a member of, you shouldn't stop there. You should identify what you can do to create a more equitable society.

"When you think everything is someone else's fault, you will suffer a lot. When you realize that everything springs only from yourself, you will learn both peace and joy." –**Dalai Lama**

Do You Suffer from a Victim Mentality?

Now for the moment of truth. It's time to find out if you suffer from a victim mentality. Take this survey and answer as honestly as possible. Then add up the points based on the number values next to your corresponding answer choices. Ready to begin?

When bad things happen to me, it's often someone else's fault.

1. Rarely
2. Sometimes
3. Usually

I find it hard to forgive people.

1. Rarely
2. Sometimes
3. Usually

I find myself asking, "Why me?" Life doesn't seem fair.

1. Rarely
2. Sometimes
3. Usually

I'm often treated poorly at work, school, or home.

1. Rarely
2. Sometimes
3. Usually

I feel it's hard to make friends because you never know whom to trust.

1. Rarely

2. Sometimes

3. Usually

I believe I have a big heart and consider myself a kind person.

1. Rarely

2. Sometimes

3. Usually

I often think that good things are supposed to happen to good people. I'm a decent person. Why don't good things happen to me more often?

1. Rarely

2. Sometimes

3. Usually

I find that when I'm feeling down, I feel a little better when I have sympathy from many people.

1. Rarely

2. Sometimes

3. Usually

I struggle with issues of low self-esteem and/or depression mainly because of how others have hurt me.

1. Rarely

2. Sometimes

3. Usually

I think I have a right to feel sorry for myself given my circumstances.

1. Rarely

2. Sometimes

3. Usually

If I act or react in a negative way, it's only because of the negative things others have done.

1. Rarely

2. Sometimes

3. Usually

Now it's time to add up your points. If your total is between 25 and 33, you suffer from a victim mentality, and it is preventing you from living the life of your dreams. Life may pass you by if you don't make some changes. If your total is between 16 and 24, you are at risk of letting a victimhood mentality sabotage your life. And if your total is between 11 and 15, you are not living your life as a victim; you are an agent of change personally and professionally. You are busy creating the life of your dreams.

Recovering from a Victim Mentality

The cold hard truth of life is that no one will care for you as much as you do. The sooner you learn this, the better. Victimhood is a cocoon from which you will never emerge a butterfly. You will be stuck in the larval phase for eternity. Is it safe? Perhaps. But you will never have the chance to fly.

———

Playing the victim triggers failure because it blocks your access to your own power.

———

It's safe to say that everyone suffers, and everyone has been a victim of unwanted circumstances. Yes, everyone. How we respond to our circumstances is what separates us.

A victim mentality is the belief that you're doomed to a life path you're helpless to change. The people who recover from difficult life circumstances are those with resilience, such as emotional mastery, mental toughness, and psychological awareness.

The good news is that you can prevent or even recover from a victim mentality. Although these strategies aren't difficult, they take work and practice, especially if you have an established pattern of victimhood. It takes time to reprogram our automatic thinking, but you can do it! Here's how to start.

- Identify what makes you feel powerless. Perhaps you lost a parent when you were young, and it turned your world upside down. That is indeed a traumatic experience that can permeate your life with grief and powerlessness. Once you've identified and processed your specific traumas and difficult experiences that left you feeling powerless, you can start to recover and reclaim your life.

- Perform acts of kindness toward yourself and others. When you're embracing victimhood, you're blinded by your pain and suffering. One of the greatest pieces of advice a mentor gave me was to volunteer. I was going through a difficult time and decided to dip my toe in the water, volunteering to coach a local hockey team. Since then, doing for others both personally and professionally has been one of the most substantial and motivating forces in my life. Be tender with yourself and then also practice giving and generosity with others. The more you give, the less you'll be stuck in "poor me."

• Stop blaming other people, groups, and institutions. There's no denying that people, groups, and institutions sometimes do us wrong. And, although it may feel like you're being singled out for more than your share of suffering, you're not. When someone does you wrong, instead of defaulting to "poor me," think about how you might respond in a way that's productive for your life goals and dreams. For example, if you're overlooked for a promotion or raise, consider approaching your boss and initiating a conversation about it. If you don't like the outcome, you can always vote with your feet and leave your job for a better position. Or, frankly, do some inner reflection on what you could be doing more of to deserve the raise in the future. People rarely spite others solely because of a personal vendetta. Usually, when someone doesn't like you, they will just highlight your shortcomings more often than others. So, instead of becoming upset, begin to fine-tune your shortcomings and perform better and faster. This way, instead of arguing your case, you are proving your worth. Not only will your boss gain respect for you, but the next time it's time for a raise, he will have nothing to say but "how much?"

• Take charge of your needs and desires. Identify what you need for a happy, healthy life and go after those things with a vengeance. Don't put someone else in charge of creating the life of your dreams. They don't have as much at stake as you do, and they may never get around to it.

• Take responsibility for the circumstances in your life. Sometimes life doesn't go as planned, and bad things happen to good people. Even if you are truly a victim of something that you didn't cause, you still must take responsibility. It won't help to try to pin it on someone else. The only person you have control over is you.

• Choose your thoughts and feelings. You can't choose everything that happens to you, but you can choose your thoughts and feelings in response to those things. Thoughts and feelings translate into behavior. Trade "I'm a victim. I can't change anything" for "I'm the primary agent of change in my life, and I can do anything I set my mind to!"

Although victimhood is trendy and may be tempting at times, it is not a healthy outlook for a fulfilling and productive life. Even if you're tempted by the rewards of victimhood, resist it at all costs. Otherwise, you'll passively watch your life go by, and you'll wake up wondering why you never attained your dreams. It is a surefire path to bitterness, disillusionment, and regret. Reject victimhood for a life of resilience, strength, fulfillment, and wonder.

CHAPTER 4

DON'T JUST HAVE A CONVERSATION; DO SOMETHING!

"There should be less talk. Take a broom and clean someone's house. That says enough." –Mother Teresa

---

A tragedy has struck somewhere in America. Perhaps it's a natural disaster, an all too common occurrence in today's world. What follows is an outpouring of thoughts and prayers on social media—people absorbing the horrific event and wanting to do or say something meaningful that relieves the collective angst and pain. But after so many devastating disasters in America and throughout the world, if thoughts and prayers were going to do anything, they would've done so by now. Thoughts and prayers are clearly not enough.

Knowing people, it's very easy to say and send stuff out into the world of nice. People want to appear charitable and kind, but they don't necessarily want to or even know how to take steps to be charitable. Although kind, thoughts and prayers are not charity. When people say, "Let me pray on it," I envy their level of faith and trust in the Lord. It requires a profound level of faith to say "I'm not going to do anything; I'm just going to pray on it." And while praying may seem active, in the world of change, it is passive. Waiting for God to handle a problem or issue is noble, but the truth is, if you just pray, things will not change except by chance. If you act on a problem or issue, you become a participant in making the world a better place.

Have you heard people say, "Let's have a conversation?" This can mean anything or nothing. It's a common phrase used by those who want to pretend they are doing something, but they don't know enough about a topic, don't think it's a worthwhile cause, or simply believe having a conversation will yield real results. It's commonly used by American politicians on both sides of the aisle. They say, "Let's have a conversation about climate change, health care, abortion, higher education, guns, the minimum wage, college tuition, transportation, crime, or the opioid crisis." The brilliance of saying we need a national conversation is that it's a way of taking a stand without taking a stand. The speaker looks compassionate, in touch, and proactive, and the key word here is "looks." There's no evidence that they are.

It is important to associate an idea with an immediate action, or, more likely than not, it will remain an idea forever. The action doesn't have to start and finish immediately. Anything is better than nothing. Nothing has ever been designed, built, and delivered just by having a conversation.

—

"Calling for dialogue is an easy way to avoid actually having one." –Jack Shafer, Politico, senior media writer

—

The Illusion of Action

While social media offers opportunities to connect digitally and communicate with people across the globe, it also gives users the feeling that they're doing something about a problem or issue when they're not. For example, let's say someone on a neighborhood list-serv posts that homeless people have been leaving heroin needles in her backyard. Then dozens of people weigh in on the homelessness problem, drug addiction, and mental illness. Some think the city should provide more shelter; others think the police force should crack down; still others think that homeless people should have greater rights and freedom. Eventually, the thread gets caustic and accusatory. Meanwhile the woman who's finding needles in her yard wants a "not in my back yard" (NIMBY) solution.

Some might argue that the discourse is productive, but if you think about it, what changed as a result of the online chatter? Probably very little. The platform gave the participants the feeling they were doing something about the problem. And the likelihood that any of the participants will take meaningful action in their community is slim. Their need to do something was fulfilled by weighing in on the problem. And the illusion of action replaces with action itself. Bottom line: Real life and potential action are all around us. Step away from your screen and do something.

"Conversations worth having energize people. They foster efficiency, fuel meaningful engagement, and generate creative possibilities." –Jackie Stavros and Cheri Torres, authors, **Conversations Worth Having**

If it's a conversation worth having, have it right now. Then once you've had it, act on it. You can have a conversation, but in this context, if it doesn't lead to action, it's not worth having. For example, many people talk about the problem of drug addiction in the U.S. A dear friend of mine struggled with heroin addiction for years, lived on the street, and was incarcerated. He was able to change his trajectory and has managed to maintain sobriety for about ten years. With his new outlook on life and the support of close friends, he has started an organization that works to help addicts and their families. He speaks with community leaders, public and private rehabilitation centers, and local citizens. Although extremely important, these conversations would be nothing without the action that follows.

Let's substitute, "It's worth a conversation" to "What's the first step that needs to be taken?" or "How can we make this happen?" In other words, just do it. Form a committee. Make a change. Do something real, but don't just sit there talking and doing nothing. Life will pass you by.

Uninterrupted, unabridged conversations lead to progress and, in turn, lead to more motivation and action. When you have a conversation with somebody, you leave feeling excited and like you can take on the world.

Worthy Conversations

Meaningful action is often preceded by conversations. But not just any old conversation; worthy conversations. What makes a conversation worth having? We've all had conversations with people who are closed, defeatist, and not action oriented. These conversations leave you feeling depleted, irritated, and depressed. The dialogue often goes around and around in an endless cycle of negativity and inaction. It's as if some people want to remain stuck and don't want you to lift them out of their comfortable ruts.

In contrast, conversations worth having are open, generative, inspiring, and action oriented. They're open in the sense that people come to the table without preconceived notions and without having made up their minds. They allow the conversation to shift their perspective and open their eyes to new ways of doing things. They're generative in that they explore ideas and solutions without judgment. The people having the conversation are inspired by the dialogue because not only do they learn something new, their perspective is also forever changed by the conversation—there is magic in the synergy of ideas and emotions. Finally, these conversations are action-oriented in that the people involved identify the best course of action and then commit to making it happen—to bringing the ideas to life.

—

Hope is for suckers.

—

Words Matter

Whenever someone uses the word *hope*, I look at them and say, "Hope is for suckers." It's my trademark line. For example, "I hope to become a realtor." You either plan to become one or you don't; but hoping will never get you there. The word *if* is also problematic. For instance, someone might say, "I'll meet your proposed deadline if I can." *If* gives you a way out, an escape hatch, the ability to bail on a commitment. To be a person of your word, you either meet your deadline or you don't meet your deadline. Another wimpy word is *try*. "I'll try to finish the project." *Try* sounds like you may or may not get the job done. It doesn't engender confidence in you.

The words you choose and the way you attack every minute of every day can affect your thinking. And thinking always precedes action. Never forget that thoughts are powerful tools that can shift the way you approach life and how you achieve your goals and dreams.

Let's power up your language with a few examples:

Replace *if* with *when*.

- "*If* I earn my master's in accounting, I will become a CPA."
- "*When* I earn my master's in accounting, I will become a CPA."

Replace *I hope* with *I will*.

- "I *hope* I can start my own business as an interior decorator."
- "I *will* start my own business as an interior decorator."

Replace *I'll try* with *I will*.

- "I'll *try* to help with your fundraiser."
- "I *will* help with your fundraiser."

The more positive the actions you take to move toward your life goals and dreams, the more your brain is conditioned to understand *who you are and what you do*. Actions fuel positive thinking, and positive thinking fuels actions. It's a beautiful, self-reinforcing equation that can transform your life. If you've been conditioned to be defeatist or noncommittal, know that it will take some time to reprogram your brain for positive thoughts and action.

"The journey of 5,000 miles begins with a single step."
–Ancient Chinese proverb

Don't get discouraged if you find yourself caught in a cycle of your old negative patterns. In short, reprogramming takes time and effort. And, like so many things in life, it takes practice.

Incremental Change Isn't Sexy

People think that they need to take drastic, dramatic steps to make change. The irony is, if you take drastic steps, you are more likely to fail. Most of the world revolves around steady, persistent, incremental change. The best way to succeed is to take one small thing and incorporate it; take the next little thing, incorporate it; and over time you're going to achieve something great. As you're making incremental progress, you may not feel like you're getting anywhere. You certainly won't feel like you're moving quickly. But if you persist, you'll discover down the road that you covered lots of ground as you plodded along—and eventually you reached the mountaintop. The 360-degree view from there will be so satisfying because only you will know the blood, sweat, and tears that went into reaching the summit. As the ancient Chinese proverb goes, "The journey of 5,000 miles begins with a single step."

Along those same lines, my grandfather had two phrases he loved to use: "Worry about the pennies and nickels, the dollar bills will take care of themselves," and "no rush, sooner or later it will be in somebody's way" (talking about his strategy on buying real estate).

Not just through these "isms," but through his actions time and time again, he highlighted the incredible value of patience and small, incremental change. Growing from humble beginnings, and from a different generation altogether, he learned what it was to survive, long before he ever had the opportunity to thrive. What began as sweeping floors in an auto repair shop turned into a small real estate empire that he could proudly call his own. And all this was done by "watching the pennies and nickels," and "waiting for it to be in somebody's way." Bottom line: Incremental change isn't sexy, but it works.

How Can You Make a Difference?

So, you've decided you have grown tired of just having conversations about doing something to make a difference in the world, and you're ready to do something. How do you choose what to do to make a difference?

When you think about the issues you're most passionate about, which ones stand out? Is there a dire need in your community for help in a specific area? Make a choice based on passion and proximity. Then just get out there and do something. You could join a nonprofit board or volunteer with a service organization. If you'd prefer to make a difference on your own, start your own organization or work solo to address a problem. Something as simple as picking up litter and trash in your community is something you could do right away without much fanfare.

Here's what it looks like in real life:

A retired woman joined an organization that goes down to the southern border of the United States—hands and boots are needed on the ground—and provides meals to refugees. It doesn't solve the issue of immigration, but it is a good example of someone who says, "I'm not going to just have a conversation; I'm going to do something to make a difference."

A woman in Boulder, Colorado, carries granola bars in her car, and when she sees a panhandler at a stoplight or stop sign, she'll roll down her window and pass them out. Although the panhandlers may prefer money for drugs or booze, she knows she's not contributing to their addictions.

A man in Indianapolis opened a food pantry for needy families. What started as mobile pantry turned into permanent pantry. They took food to inner-city churches, and the people would come in and help themselves to the food. It became a lifelong passion for him.

An 11-year-old boy made sure homeless men and women kept warm during winter. He collected blankets for people in need in Michigan. The goal was to collect and pass out 800 blankets, but he more than doubled that. The final tally was 1,626 blankets.

Let's revisit the problem we started with in this chapter—dealing with the devastation of a natural disaster. Natural disasters are a great example, because no one is to blame. But with any negative outcome, the human mind immediately wants to make complex problems such as this easier to solve. We aim to put things in boxes and create easy-to-manage, black-and-white scenarios. For example, some Americans think something needs to be done about climate change and that it is the undisputed cause of natural disasters. Others cast blame on the efforts (or lack thereof) of companies and governments sending aid, all the while not donating their own time or resources. Instead of using outrage as a commodity, use the human capital you already possess. Rather than continuing to have a conversation, because, obviously, just talking about it doesn't accomplish anything, take action, such as:

- *Donate to on-the-ground relief organizations.* In the immediate aftermath, thousands of people will require urgent and ongoing medical assistance, food, clean water, shelter, and more. Emergency responders and relief organizations will also work on repairing essential infrastructure like water and sanitation systems, power plants, hospitals, homes, and roads.

- *Support food banks and temporary housing organizations.* In addition to relief organizations, you can support food pantries and shelters that have long operated in affected areas. These organizations might have experienced damage from the disaster in the form of flooded or destroyed buildings and displaced personnel—and they, too, will need help recovering.

- *Donate to crowdfunding campaigns.* For all the essential work done by government agencies and nonprofits, countless people will fall through the cracks and be plunged into debt and hardship as a result of the storm. Some people will lose their homes and businesses. Others will have to pay for costly medical procedures and funeral expenses.

Most of us are guilty of having conversations that go nowhere, even with the best of intentions. To rally after a conversation takes focus, motivation, and determination. If you feel a conversation is worth having, have it with proactive people as soon as you can. Then, once you've had it, formulate a plan and do something. Remember: you can have a conversation, but if it doesn't lead to action, it's not worth having. And try not to fall into the trap of dead-end digital chatter about problems and issues that never leaves the screen. Don't let another day go by without being an active participant in our busy, thriving, vibrant world that needs your creative ideas and solutions.

CHAPTER 5

PREVENTING DIGITAL DISTRACTIONS

We've all been there. You're working on an important deadline, something catches your attention on YouTube, and an hour later, you realize you went down a rabbit hole checking out your favorite musical artist or tunes from your high school years—the soundtrack of your youth. The internet and social media are like seductive sirens forever singing a song of temptation. And, let's face it, it's hard to ward off the impulse to engage. Testing our willpower, we often fall short and surrender to the urge when we have so many other things to do. You may be thinking there's no harm in plugging in—everyone else is doing it. Wait until you see what the research shows about our brains going digital as often as we do. But first, a story.

A few years ago, I was studying like crazy for a professional exam. At around 2:00 p.m. every day, I hit a wall and couldn't think efficiently anymore. I tried to push past it, but there was nothing I could do to break through to the other side. I realized I only have a certain amount of cognitive bandwidth each day. If I use half my bandwidth on social media and other digital distractions, I'm wasting a lot of my bandwidth on useless stuff. The less bandwidth I waste on digital distractions, the more I have for productive thinking and actions.

The bottom line is, each day we have a limited amount of mental capacity. And we are using so much of our cognitive bandwidth on useless information from social media, memes, vlogs, gaming videos, and YouTube videos, simply because of how accessible they are. Researchers estimate we've created more information in the last ten years than in all human history. Just in the last two years, 90 percent of the world's data was generated.

Information scientists have put numbers to this. In 2011, Americans took in five times as much information every day as they did in 1986—the equivalent of 174 newspapers. During our leisure time, we process thirty-four gigabytes, or 100,000 words, every day!

The upside is that the internet presents a platform for limitless learning of new information and complex processes. It's as if search engines are the genie in a bottle, granting our every wish, and the search engines are the new schools. If you have a problem or issue to solve, the solution is just an internet search away! If you want to learn a new skill, jump on YouTube. So, it's not all bad. In fact, it can be very good, if harnessed properly. But that's the problem: an overwhelming majority of us are controlled by our digital devices and not the other way around. For example, we've all seen new parents who, instead of paying attention to their babies, are glued to their phones. Or a couple on a date, when they should be spending time getting to know each other, are instead staring at their phones across the table from each other.

According to a study published recently in the *Journal of the Association for Consumer Research*, a smartphone can tax its user's cognition simply by sitting next to them on a table, or just being anywhere in the same room. It finds that a smartphone can demand its user's attention even when the person isn't using it or consciously thinking about it. It's like we're big kids, and a smartphone is an enticing toy. When our phone is nearby, we can't not play with it.

The human brain is powerful—capable of incredible feats—but the current barrage of data and information is more than our brains can handle. The conscious mind can pay attention to only a few things at once. If you exceed that, your judgment is impaired and your focus frayed. Our brains are on overdrive processing the images, data, and information coming at us, so we pay a price: we struggle to separate the significant from the trivial, and all this information processing leaves us exhausted and depleted.

Neuroscientists maintain the digital age takes a toll on our cognitive abilities. Our ability to concentrate, to think deeply, to be creative, to have room in our minds for free thinking is overtaxed in a world where technology streams compete for our attention. Experts note there's a direct correlation between the widespread use of smartphones and a decrease in productivity. Our ability to focus is not just essential for productivity but for our mental health.

Vetting News and Information in the Age of Fake News

Not only is the amount of information a problem in the digital age, but the quality of information has become a huge problem. With the advent of the internet and social media, we've seen the proliferation of false news stories or fake news. Fake news is news, stories, or hoaxes generated to deliberately misinform or deceive readers. This content, which can look like it is from trusted websites, is written to influence views, advance a political agenda, or cause confusion. We've seen in this era of fake news that people aren't particularly skilled at spotting fake news and vetting sources. To be an informed citizen and a savvy consumer, you need to know the truth. How can you separate fact from fiction?

1. Assess the publisher's credibility by checking its publication history.

2. Go to Wikipedia to see that the sources and citations are legitimate.

3. Verify information with fact-checking websites, such as Snopes or Factcheck.org.

Culture of Distraction

A culture of distraction takes a toll both professionally and personally. We waste time, attention, and energy on relatively unimportant information and interactions, staying busy but producing little of value. People who regularly juggle several streams of content do not pay attention, memorize, or manage their tasks as well as those who focus on one thing at a time. The result is reduced productivity and engagement.

Opportunity Cost

What do you pay when you let your devices control you and not the other way around? You pay with your dreams. Before you think I'm being overly dramatic, consider this: when you get sucked into the digital world by one of the many temptations—and there are many—you sacrifice all the actions you don't take to pursue your dreams in creating your future. Perhaps you sacrifice your relationships with your spouse, kids, or friends when you're busy YouTubing or Instagramming instead of engaging with them. Perhaps you sacrifice work on the small business you've always dreamed of launching or the hobby that makes you feel truly alive.

You might also be paying with your health and wellness. If you're using up your bandwidth on—let's face it—trivial, unimportant stuff, you may be increasing your stress load, leaving your brain and body wired, frazzled, and depleted. This can affect the food and beverage choices you make—more caffeine in the morning for a much-needed boost and more alcohol at night to help you wind down. You might also reach for more sugar and simple carbs for an uptick in energy. And all of this is going to affect your sleep unless you're a rock-star sleeper who can snooze through anything. Do you get the picture? A digitally drained you will not be the best you.

Remember: just because the digital siren is singing her beautiful song of temptation, doesn't mean you need to respond to it.

Three questions are begging to be asked. I'd recommend taking an honest look at yourself and your digital engagement by answering these three questions:

1. How is your digital life serving your real life?

2. How is your digital behavior interfering with the life of your dreams?

3. How can your digital life change so you can create the life of your dreams?

Digital Distractions Test

Let's dive deeper into your personal level of digital distraction. This survey created by Dr. David Greenfield from the Center for Internet and Technology Addiction will help you determine whether you are too digitally connected. Ready to begin?

1. Do you find yourself spending more and more time online or on your digital devices (computer, laptop, tablet, or smartphone) than you realize?

Yes

No

2. Do you find yourself mindlessly passing time on a regular basis by staring at your smartphone, tablet, or computer even when there might be better or more productive things to do? And do you seem to lose track of time when on any of these devices?

Yes

No

3. Do you find yourself spending more time with virtual friends as opposed to real people?

Yes

No

4. Has the amount of time you spend on your digital devices and the internet been increasing?

Yes

No

5. Do you secretly wish you could be a little less wired or connected to your devices such as your smartphone, laptop, tablet, internet, etc.?

Yes

No

6. Do you sleep with your smartphone under your pillow or next to your bed regularly?

Yes

No

7. Do you find yourself viewing and answering texts, tweets, and emails at all hours of the day and night—even when it means interrupting other things you are doing?

Yes

No

8. Do you text, email, tweet, or surf while driving or doing other similar activities that require your focused attention and concentration?

Yes

No

9. Do you feel your use of technology decreases your productivity at times?

Yes

No

10. Do you find yourself feeling somewhat ill-at-ease or uncomfortable when you accidentally leave your phone or other internet digital device in the car or at home, if you have no service, or if it is broken?

Yes

No

11. Do you feel reluctant to be without your smartphone or other digital devices, even for a short time; when you leave the house, do you always have your smartphone or other digital device with you?

Yes

No

12. When you eat meals is your smartphone always part of the table place setting?

Yes

No

If you answered "Yes" to more than three or four of these questions, you would likely benefit from unplugging or at least managing your digital distractions better. Here are several ideas for doing that. Mix and match, try a couple, or try them all!

Unplug from Devices and Plug into Life: Approaches for Preventing Digital Distraction

Despite what the experts say about what our brains are capable of in the digital age, you may remain unconvinced that digital distraction is a problem for you. Whether you're convinced or not, take these strategies for a test-drive and see if you notice a difference in your focus, productivity, and connection to others. It may make you aware that what you thought was working well for you is not optimal for your personal and professional life. Control the digital distractions and information overload rather than letting them control you.

How do you do that, exactly?

Cultivate Self-Awareness

To determine a healthy amount of digital interaction for you, first cultivate self-awareness. I'd recommend starting with a trial-and-error approach. Begin by not changing your behavior, but just noticing your patterns of digital device use. There are tools that can help you evaluate this, such Screen Time in Settings on iPhones. After you observe, then start to control your use, such as less checking your phone throughout the day, less time on social media, and less scrolling through the highlight reels of people's lives. As you scale back, do you notice a change in the levels of your mental and emotional energy? How does it feel to be less digitally distracted?

Establish a Distraction-Free Zone

Even though you may think you're a master of the digital realm, constantly switching between email, texting, the internet, and social media shreds your attention and robs you of time and focus. Cal Newport, a computer scientist at Georgetown University, talks of *deep work* when characterizing professional activities performed in a state of distraction-free concentration. He warns of seemingly small interruptions that appear harmless by themselves but, in totality, inflict serious injury to deep work. Cultivate an awareness of the difference between what Newport calls *shallow work* (heavy on digital distraction) and a deeper state of undivided attention.

Schedule Checking

It is tempting to check all your incoming—texts, emails, news alerts, etc.—every few minutes, but this behavior dilutes your concentration and compromises your cognitive capacity. Even if you think you're good at simultaneously checking and managing distractions, you're not. Why? Because no one is. So, consider scheduling times to check your incoming—maybe once every couple of hours. If you're engrossed in a project that demands deep concentration, check even less—just a couple times a day. If this sounds drastic, it probably means you need to do this even more than most. Give it a try and watch your mind recover from fragmented attention.

Go Old School

Remember that the device in your hand can be used to connect with people through conversation. I talk on the phone to as many people possible, sometimes just to say "hi." How many people, who are not closely related and who don't need anything, call you just to say, "How are you? I was thinking of you. I hope you're doing well. Give my love to the family." Make a habit of connecting with your contacts. It may make someone's day, and it will definitely make yours.

Get Off Your Couch

Even though you may have become one with your couch in the digital age, you must get off your couch to create a life. No, seriously. Go out into the community and have face-to-face interactions. Research shows that positive interactions with strangers boosts your happiness quotient. If everything is delivered to your house, you will become a miserable shut-in.

Fewer and fewer people can look someone in the eye and work with them on a real human level. Since that skill set is scarcer than in previous generations, emotional intelligence (EQ) is becoming increasingly important. Just like in economics, it's a supply and demand thing. Cultivating emotional intelligence not only will make you happier, it will set you apart from the pack.

Wander and Wonder

Our minds greatly benefit from downtime during which we are doing nothing and letting our minds out of their cages. And by doing nothing, I don't mean being on your device. Social media isn't downtime. It's not regenerating you. It's not refueling you. It's still fidgeting. Psychologically speaking, staring at your phone for an hour on a social media site stimulates your brain, releasing endorphins and chemicals without allowing for a brain break.

When I speak of doing nothing, I mean letting your mind wander and wonder. Daydreaming allows ideas to form into dreams and realities. Downtime for our minds is essential for creativity and generative ideas.

Rest and Refresh

Nathaniel Kleitman identified a ninety-minute work-rest cycle for our brains when we're asleep and awake. To work with your brain's natural rhythms, take a rest-and-refresh break every hour and a half, especially if you're stressing your brain with multitasking and technology.

Given that each day we have a limited amount of mental capacity, being strategic about how we use that capacity is essential to a life well-lived. We are fortunate to live in an age with a world of information at our fingertips and with digital devices that give us access to that world. We must protect ourselves by structuring our lives in such a way that our digital tools enhance rather than detract from our quality of life. If our devices pull us into the 24-7 universe of posting, commenting, liking, tweeting, messaging, Instagramming, and YouTubing, we'll have lost the battle. If we pace ourselves, mindfully engage, and keep our distractions at a minimum, we'll productively coexist with our digital devices.

CHAPTER 6

TRUTH-SEEKING:
THE NEW IQ MEASURE IN THE
DIGITAL AGE

―――――

"Whatever I have accepted until now as most true has come to me through my senses. But occasionally I have found that they have deceived me, and it is unwise to trust completely those who have deceived us even once." –Rene Descartes

―――――

A recent survey found that just 66 percent of young adults aged 18 to 24 years old have "always believed the world is round." That's 34 percent of Americans who believe the world is flat, last propagated by religious beliefs in Middle Ages. The idea of a spherical Earth was proposed by Pythagoras around 500 BCE and validated by Aristotle a couple centuries later.

Reading this statistic, you might conclude that the 34 percent of Americans who believe the Earth is flat—flat-Earthers—are just plain dumb. But people don't fall for fake news simply because they're dumb. With news and information coming at us at breakneck speed in newsfeeds on Facebook, Instagram, texts, and emails, we need to pace ourselves and conserve our mental energy, so we skim headlines, articles, newsfeeds, and social media threads, making snap judgments and drawing speedy conclusions. We face a tsunami of misinformation, half-truths, and advertising appearing as news and opinion that seems fact-based. It takes time and effort to vet news and information. And most of us simply don't have either in our fast-paced world. Given our need for expediency, we tend to look for articles and posts that seem to be real and ones that align with our beliefs. And research indicates that six out of ten people share headlines on social media without reading the article.

Fake News

What is fake news? The *Oxford English Dictionary* defines it as "news that conveys or incorporates false, fabricated, or deliberately misleading information, or that is characterized as or accused of doing so." Fake news is a feature of our "post-truth" era, which the *OED* describes as "relating to or denoting circumstances in which objective facts are less influential in shaping public opinion than appeals to emotion and personal belief."

This current fake news era refers to the social trend in which people tend to believe what they feel should be correct based on personal beliefs rather than concrete evidence and fact, even when contradictory facts are presented. In other words, we tend to confirm our biases. Is fake news a new phenomenon? Not by a long stretch. The term was first used in the 1800s, when newspapers owned by media magnate William Randolph Hearst fabricated stories about invented battles in the Spanish-American war. Back then, the muckrakers, reform-minded progressive-era journalists, adopted the term to expose large news institutions when they provided coverage slanted toward the corporations who subsidized them.

The Pew Research Center published a study demonstrating that a majority of Americans have difficulty distinguishing between fact and opinion. Only 26 percent of adults correctly identified five factual statements as such, and only 35 percent were able to do the same for five opinion statements.

A factor that further contributes to the misinformation epidemic is where Americans get their news and information. According to another Pew research study, in 2017, two-thirds of American adults got their news from only social media. Social media is notably less reliable than other forms of digital content. This trend has resulted in news being disseminated that is inaccurate, skewed, biased, fabricated, and even outlandish. For example, researchers from Texas Tech University believe they've isolated YouTube videos as ground zero for the spread of flat-earth theories. In other words: if you see it, you tend to believe it.

The Poison of Persuasion

Imagine you are in a business meeting, discussing a critical issue, weighing the pros and cons of a decision that will impact the bottom line. One meeting attendee speaks quickly, forcefully, and passionately. She is on one side of the issue. A second attendee speaks slowly and softly and is more measured in his approach. He is on the other side of the issue. Which one are you more likely to believe and be persuaded by? Research indicates that you are more likely to believe the first speaker because her speaking style is more persuasive. But research shows that she is not necessarily more likely to have the best information or be correct. She just appears to be more of an expert because of her tone and style. It's important to remember that just because a so-called expert is passionately presenting something, it doesn't mean that the information they're presenting is fact-based. They could be uninformed or lying through their teeth, but their presentation style is so persuasive, you believe it. In the case of the two meeting presenters, what if the more understated speaker has the critical information your company needs to survive, but because the more persuasive speaker has more influence, your company decides to base its decision on her approach? Your company will likely suffer the consequences of using the opinion of the most persuasive person in its decision-making process.

Now imagine you've tuned into a news show. The anchor is persuasive, passionate, at times fervently so, touting positions that sound convincing because the anchor is so confident. Now imagine that same person is claiming that humans never went to the moon—that all the so-called moon photos were staged with actors in astronaut suits. Even though there is indisputable evidence that humans did in fact go to the moon, the anchor is so darned sure of himself, a seed of doubt is planted in your mind. He so persuasively argues that the moon landings were fake that you become a moon-hoax conspiracy theorist. You were poisoned by persuasion.

The Importance of Truth-Seeking

In this era of fake news, hoaxes, and scams, the ability to discern the truth is more important than ever. Truth-seeking acuity is one's ability to identify factual information and tell noise from substance.

66

With the minefield of distraction and fabricated news, information, and profiles, we need a level head and truth-seeking acuity to survive. We must have the confidence and hunger to search for truth in the world, not simply consume facts and answers as they are packaged and fed to us. So often, the information being pushed comes with a well-honed agenda to influence your thinking and behavior, whether it's to purchase a given product, submit to indoctrination, or adopt a given political point of view. You must master the art of critical thinking to vet information.

Critical Thinking in the Digital Age

If it's on the internet, it must be true—right? Even though you might laugh at that assertion, you're probably not immune to the stealthy manipulation of the web. Some experts estimate 40 percent of the internet content is fake; a lot of it is bot activity. For example, for a period of time in 2013, the *Times* reported this year, a full half of YouTube traffic was bots masquerading as people.

It can be tempting to assume a couch-slouch position and become a passive consumer of news and information, scouring the web for content that aligns with our beliefs, outlooks, and perspectives. We must fight this temptation and challenge our assumptions and prejudices. Pay special attention to the beliefs that evoke an intense emotional response and prompt you to attack others on the web. Your passionately held position might just benefit from an objective examination of the facts.

Our inability to separate truth from fiction on the internet, and social media in particular, is essential to remaining informed citizens and savvy consumers. With the scourge of fake news, clickbait, and deep fakes (realistic-looking videos of bogus events), people are worried about the future of democracy. We have plenty of evidence indicating that bad actors are interfering in elections by creating millions of bots and spewing propaganda on social media. It is not overstating the case to say that our difficulty in discerning falsehoods threatens civilized society and its democratic institutions.

Distracted and Manipulated in the Digital Age

After reading this section heading, you might think: *Oh, I'm not a sucker!* But does this sound familiar? You hop onto the web to research something for a work deadline. Ads, articles, and other clickbait content pops up, and before you know it, you are spending lots of time on Instagram, Snapchat, or Facebook—something that has no legitimate impact on your life or intended focus. Whether you're looking to see what an old friend or ex is doing, shopping on Amazon, or looking to plan your next vacation, it's not what you set out to do when you opened your phone or laptop. You look at the time and find you've just spent thirty minutes unintentionally distracted.

How did this happen? How could you have been so unfocused? It's all according to plan. Websites permit advertisers to lure you in with clickbait. (You're the fish. The irresistible content is the worm.) According to Wikipedia, clickbait is a form of false advertising that uses hyperlink text or a thumbnail link designed to attract attention and entice users to follow that link to access the piece of online content. It is typically deceptive, sensationalized, or misleading. When websites use clickbait, they typically value getting clicks over producing quality information. This means they do not care if they waste your time with mediocre content. After clickbait pulls you in, their algorithms see to it that you're served up your favorite things. What is an algorithm? Some algorithms are machine-learning systems designed to learn what interests users based on their online activities, then serve them more relevant content. The free apps and content you accessed are paid for by advertisers who desperately seek your eyeballs. Your attention is worth a fortune to them in advertising and subscription revenue.

Newsfeed algorithms attempt to show you more of what you already like, pushing you into a tighter and tighter corner, basically shrinking your world and worldview. And before you know it, by constant reinforcement mechanisms, you're entrenched in your stance in an echo chamber of like-minded people. Our increasingly polarized country is being shaped in part by these algorithms.

For the sake of argument, let's continue to look at the flat Earth example—no matter how insane that might sound. Let's say a naive YouTuber happens upon a persuasive flat-Earther video. The YouTube algorithm will then recommend more flat-Earther videos—including ones with celebrities—that claim to debunk round-Earth science. Convinced by the seemingly factual round-Earth debunking, the YouTuber becomes a diehard flat-Earther, preaching the gospel to everyone he or she meets. The same goes for religion, politics, news, and any other content you may consume. Although the debate about a flat Earth doesn't have a large impact on the daily lives of many, these topics do. And continuing to consume biased information will lead to an increasingly divided people.

———

"Certain algorithms pull you toward the things you already know, believe, or like, and they push away everything else. Push back. It shouldn't be this way. Opening your eyes and seeing things in a new way can be a revolutionary act."
–Tim Cook, CEO, Apple

———

Become the Master of Your Feed: Digital Media Literacy

Apple CEO Tim Cook, in a commencement speech at Tulane University, urged students to push back against the algorithms in social media that perpetuate what they already believe. We would all benefit from heeding his warning. But what should those of us who aren't tech geeks do when we fail to grasp the back-end programming that's manipulating us? How do we ensure that our newsfeeds don't serve up increasingly misleading or one-sided content?

To outsmart social media algorithms, follow these steps:

1. Don't limit your news to a Facebook or Twitter newsfeed. Try Feedly, a less popularity-driven platform.

2. Use apps and extensions like Freedom and uBlock Origin to hide dubious web links and ads.

3. Install advertising blockers or filters on your digital devices. They block online advertising in a web browser or an application.

4. Be wary of websites that rely on Google ads. It's in their best interest to get you to click on more ads, and thus their content is more likely to be questionable.

5. When you use YouTube, don't log in; that way, you'll be less likely to get recommended videos.

6. Uninstall Facebook from your phone: Just use it on your laptop, and install "Facebook News Feed Eradicator" and "Facebook Demetricator" browser plugin/extensions.

Vetting News and Information in the Fake News Era

So, after reading this chapter, you're convinced that you want to be an informed citizen and a savvy information consumer and put digital content to the truth test. This will slow you down a bit but will heighten your perspective and worldview. What steps can you take to parse fact from fiction?

- Identify news sources that are reliable, fair, and well-researched by checking their credentials.
- Determine if multiple sources are reporting a given story in more or less the same way. If not, it's probably fake news.
- Evaluate the publisher's credibility by checking its publication history.
- Check to see if the author of a given piece is real and credible.
- Go to Wikipedia to see that sources and citations are legitimate.
- Use fact-checking websites, such as Snopes, Factcheck.org, or TruthOrFiction.com.

Humans have always needed to live with a healthy dose of caution to protect themselves, their families, and society. People and organizations with their self-serving agendas prey upon those who are unaware of their schemes. The internet is being used as a propaganda tool by many to shape thought and behavior. People and groups with nefarious intentions can do harm to our democracy. Without a keen awareness of these forces and how they operate, we can easily fall prey to their manipulation. The more we seek the truth by vetting news and information, the better off we'll be.

CHAPTER 7

HANDLING LOVE AND LOSS

———

"When the sun has set, no candle can replace it."
–George R.R. Martin

———

How we handle love and loss is arguably the most important thing in our lives. Love is a powerful force that binds us to people, motivates us to make a difference in the lives of others, and helps us thrive. Love makes the impossible possible. In this way, there's a certain magic to love. Loss is inevitable in that all things must end—including love—so no one escapes the clutches of loss and grief, not even the most isolated among us. In the same way that love makes our heart swell, loss pierces our blossoming heart and makes us feel that we may never love again. Or that we may never stop feeling the pain.

If you look at your own life and those around you, you'll discover that how we react to love and loss is a major force that shapes who we become. The decisions you make in the midst of a loss, when your emotions are running high, set in motion your life's path. The difference between successful and unsuccessful people is how they channel grief, loss, and pain in their lives. As the saying goes, life is 10 percent what happens and 90 percent how you react to it. Mindset is everything; it determines our thoughts and actions.

Let's face it. Life can be tough on everyone, and it's easy to let difficult times consume or even destroy you. We all know people who, like a besieged ship at sea, let life's travails toss them around. And they're all too eager to play the victim. This is the easy way out in that it doesn't require determination, imagination, and risk in transforming hardship. It doesn't require brushing oneself off and trying again and again. It doesn't require putting it all on the line. And as a bonus, you can garner sympathy for your hard life. But the risk of this approach is stagnation, depression, and bitterness. And the ultimate consequence is dying without having lived the life of your dreams.

Successful people are hardship and loss ninjas. They understand that life is filled with beginnings and endings and lots of tedious middles. They don't let life have the last word. Ever. Life deals a blow, and they hit back. Life knocks them down, and they get back up. From the outside, it may look like these people have it easier, but the truth is they have their eye on the prize and are determined to rally, learn, grow, and emerge triumphant. They don't stop until they succeed.

———

"Our greatest weakness lies in giving up. The most certain way to success is always to try just one more time." –**Thomas Edison**

———

What allows these people to succeed? They realize that what's important is not what happens to them in their lives but how they react. The way someone responds to the cards life deals them is what shapes their feelings, actions, and results. In other words, they choose how to frame their perspective.

Here's an example. My grandfather came from very humble beginnings. Growing up in Rochester, New York, and having dropped out of school by 13 to help provide for the family, he eventually found himself in the auto repair business. After starting work as a rank-and-file employee, he began to save and purchase real estate. His famous line was, "Eventually, it's going to get in somebody's way." This was in reference to purchasing land in areas he felt would see business expansion in the near future. Completely self-taught, he eventually created a real estate business that would provide his family with the life he always desired. His story, like so many others in America, shows the benefit of not rolling over but standing up and fighting.

The Truth about Love

Love is a transformative force; it opens you up to so many things you might not otherwise be receptive to. Being enamored opens your mind to different ways of seeing and being. Your beloved can say something you might ordinarily take issue with or write off, but because you love that person, you take time to listen or wonder why they said that. And especially in the beginning of a healthy love relationship, you're on cloud nine; this new love inspires you to think and act in ways you've never considered before. You feel like this person is the key to your happiness; they're all you need.

But always remember that no one cares about your happiness as much as you. You're the only person responsible for your happiness. Your friends and family cheer your relationship on, saying things like, "Go for it. It's great stuff! We're happy for you." All true. But there is also the hard work of sustaining and maintaining a positive relationship over time.

Your loved one can do things to make you happy, but you're still ultimately responsible. You've probably seen a person in a relationship do something really nice for their significant other, and their partner's response is negative because they're in a bad place. Perhaps they're angry or sad. As a result, the person who did something thoughtful may be bummed out, having expected a completely different response. Both people are responsible for their own well-being. Expecting an outside fix is an exercise in futility.

Another example is breaking up after two months with someone who's really into you. You're not responsible for their happiness; your job is to be honest with them. Of course, it's easier said than done, and you'll experience short-term pain for a long-term gain.

There's no denying that love is the most confusing, ever-changing emotion. If anyone were to identify the formula—how to get love and keep it—they'd be the richest, most famous person in the history of the world.

Love in friendships and family relationships isn't any easier. We all have expectations for our friends and family members that they may or may not know about. And when those expectations aren't met, we may think they let us down because they don't love us enough, when really, it's just that our friend or family member didn't know what we expected of them. As much as someone may love us, mind-reading isn't part of the package of love. Communicating expectations is critical; without doing so, our faulty assumptions and dashed expectations can taint an otherwise strong connection and erode our relationship.

When it comes to expressing love, many people are scared to tell each other how they feel. I think it's important to share your feelings with loved ones. To say "I love you" is so valuable, yet underrated. Whenever I talk to those who matter most, I try to share my love for them. This is especially significant to me because many men in my family have lived to be just 52 or 53. So, I don't know how long anyone's going to be here, especially me. And I'd have no regrets if I died tomorrow because I live every day to fullest extent possible. The people in my life know that. Although I'm ultra-focused on achieving my dreams, if someone called me right now and needed me, I'd hop in a car or on a plane and show up for them. They know they're my priority.

Still, love eventually leads to loss. If you decide to love, you need to be prepared to lose; it's one of life's many tradeoffs. People don't usually associate these two things, and with good reason. They might not take the risk to love if they thought about the gut-wrenching grief that often accompanies the loss of a loved one—whether through growing apart, a breakup, or death. Similarly, thinking about death all the time while living would strike fear in the hearts of most of us and lead to an anxious existence.

The Truth about Loss

What you discover when you experience loss, especially the loss of a loved one, is how little time people have to console you. And how the world will keep on turning whether we like it or not. We would like people to stop and notice that our world has dramatically changed and will never be the same. Although they might share some condolences and choice sentiments, they don't get the depth of our loss. It's not that people are heartless; it's just that they're not walking in our shoes at that moment. Of course, those people will have their losses and, in turn, want others to show up for them. They'll have the same feeling that grieving is a pretty solitary process.

If you mention to your friends how much you still miss a loved one who has passed, they're not going to stop you from talking about it. But, at the same time, you can't expect others—your best friend or even your siblings—to be on the same level of grief as you are because everybody is different. That doesn't mean they don't care, but in some ways, it means they have moved on.

The most individualized, caring attention you will get in life is after the death of someone you love. Even in this situation, the longest anyone will check in and care is about three to four weeks. People who don't realize this simple truth often keep looking for attention from others—through no fault of their own—and find they must continue to manufacture sadness to get the attention they need.

What's going on?

In America, we don't really do death. So many things in this country are framed in terms of winning and losing; death is often seen as losing and not a naturally occurring part of life. Every organism is born and dies. So, why are we not able to talk about something that is a universal experience? Perhaps our death denial means that we don't want to acknowledge death or the accompanying persistent grief. When someone dies, loved ones not only lose a cherished friend or family member, but they lose a part of themselves. This is not something that is easily overcome. In fact, it will change the grieving person in profound ways forever.

Since my dad died, I've talked about him every day of my life. He will have an impact on me forever, and it has intensified since he died. By talking to his friends and our family members, I get to see the man he was through their eyes. A person can have a profound impact on the lives of so many around them. I've learned from his accomplishments, just as much as his mistakes. Not everyone takes the time to appreciate both in people.

My loss was meaningful in the way it shaped me. It was also anxiety-producing in the sense that my mom needed somebody to help her. At the same time, I realized the role my dad and grandfathers played in the family—they were the answer men in that everyone called them with their questions and concerns. With my dad's absence, the void became painfully obvious. Was I going to be the one to step up?

I said to myself, *my mom is scared. She doesn't know exactly what to do, and I have no answers for her.* I started thinking about how I could get the answers to her questions. My job as a financial advisor has allowed me to educate myself so that I became the guy with the answers. Mom always tells me how happy she is that she can call me and I'll have the answer. I don't know if she realizes it or not, but that's why I chose my career path. I think it worked.

Reflecting on love and loss has made me a better friend, family member, and human being. When you think about these things, you become more aware of who you are and what you're really about. Until you can define who you are, you're just wandering through life. Wandering for a time is OK—even recommended—but if you wander too long, you become filled with angst, and you might grasp for the wrong things out of anxiety.

———

"I can't change the direction of the wind, but I can adjust my sails to always reach my destination." –**Jimmy Dean**

———

Love and loss are inextricably linked. If you love—whether it's a person, an animal, a place, an experience—you will experience loss. If only we could freeze time at the height of loving someone or something. Then our experience of loving could be everlasting. But that's not how life works. It ebbs and flows—it giveth and taketh away. People who thrive don't necessarily have more love and less loss. Instead, they have figured out how to learn from loss and move on, embracing life as they go. Even if they're blindsided by a loss, they rely on well-honed coping strategies to keep going. That's the difference between successful and unsuccessful people; successful people never give up, no matter how much they loved or lost.

CHAPTER 8

DOING WHAT YOU LOVE DOESN'T HAVE TO LEAVE YOU BROKE OR DRIVE YOU CRAZY

Do what you love and you'll never work a day in your life. Do what you love, the money will follow. Are these common refrains about work, career, and making a living even true?

Well, yes and no.

When people give this kind of career guidance, it's well-intentioned, but their advice is more often than not misguided. Maybe these advice-givers were among the fortunate few who are able to align their passions with earning a living. Or maybe the people doling out the advice never had to test the job market because they had money from other sources.

We've all heard versions of the following equation: Passion + Career = Happiness and Prosperity. But here's the truth: You might identify your passion, pursue it, and then discover that doing what you love for work turns your passion into a grind. Or perhaps doing what you love may feed your soul but not your body. Let's take a look at this flawed career advice and temper it with more realistic guidance. It is possible to do what you love without having it drive you crazy and leave you broke—with some conditions and caveats.

Do What You Love and You'll Never Work a Day in Your Life

Do what you love, and you'll never work a day in your life. Wouldn't this be nice if it were true? But work is work no matter how you slice it. Even if you love what you do, your job will sometimes be arduous, tiring, frustrating, and, well, just a four-letter word: work.

Let's consider this first bit of career advice with an example. Tina loved dancing and teaching dance, so she decided to quit her day job and purchased a dance studio. It seemed like a dream come true—at first. She was teaching, choreographing, and leading a dance troupe. Then reality set in. She faced marketing, promoting, bookkeeping, and scrambling to find substitute teachers when her teachers were sick, injured, or just flaking out. Her income was dependent upon a schedule of full, thriving classes. Tina had to hustle to fill class slots with highly skilled substitutes when teachers bailed. Slowly she found herself in a quagmire of small business challenges related to dance, but she was no longer doing what she loved: teaching and dancing.

Her love for dance was whittling away, and she wondered: *why did I choose this in the first place? It's killing me.* She decided to structure her business to maximize dancing and teaching while minimizing the tasks she didn't love. Her profit margins were slim, so she decided to bring on employees with trades. In exchange for dance classes, she hired front desk people, a bookkeeper, and a web designer. That way, she wasn't paying wages out of her dance studio income. She made sure she was teaching and dancing more than doing the business end of things, and she achieved a balance that brought her much happiness.

Do What You Love, the Money Will Follow

In 99 percent of cases, *do what you love, the money will follow* doesn't ring true. It's almost like saying "eat whatever you want, and the weight loss will follow." Ask anyone who is in great shape: much of what is needed to maintain fitness is not fun. Most people don't enjoy waking up early and exercising, or not eating the food they want. They do it because the feeling of being in shape and healthy outweighs the small sacrifices to make it happen. This is not to say that enjoying your work doesn't help bring about more productivity, but your love for something does not correlate to whether or not you can make a living at it. The phrase should be changed to *do what it takes, and the money will follow*. So often in life, we need to compromise to achieve long-term happiness. Just like we compromise in relationships, we need to compromise with ourselves.

Consider Andrew. He loves writing fiction, so he quit his teaching job to go for broke in the publishing world. He pursued book deal after book deal, all to no avail. He was blowing through his savings in pursuit of his dream. Eventually, he landed a book deal with an advance of $30,000, but he was already $25,000 in debt. Andrew's book never earned out, and he eventually returned to teaching and a full-time salary with benefits. He concluded that, as a writer, he must have a day job; he still had to pay rent and put food on the table. With job security as a teacher, he carved out time to write in the early mornings and on weekends and continued to pursue publishing deals. Only, this time, he wasn't dependent upon income from his books to live, so he felt less stress around pursuing what he loved. Andrew returned to doing what he loved by designing a life that worked for him.

———

The average American spends one-third of their lives at work, or 90,000 hours over their lifetime.

———

Pay-to-Play Society

We live in a pay-to-play society. Unless you inherit or marry into money, you will have to pay to participate every day of your life, which means generating an income stream until you retire. For most people, this means working thirty to forty years at a minimum. The average American spends one-third of their life or 90,000 hours at work over their lifetime. And considering that you spend another third of your life sleeping, that leaves the remaining third for family, friends, chores, and fun. Your happy/work quotient gets squeezed by life's necessities. So, of course, it makes sense to choose your career wisely. The risks of disliking your work include depression, anxiety, insomnia, substance abuse, and illness. Work defines us, so when we aren't happy with our work, other areas of our life suffer. Yet more than 70 percent of workers say they don't feel satisfied with their career choices. How many times have you heard about people who end up sick, depressed, divorced, or abusing substances because they're unhappy with their careers? What if they liked their work instead? Wouldn't improving how people choose their careers greatly boost the well-being of American society?

Here's career advice tempered with a dose of reality so you don't end up crashing and burning by designing an unworkable life.

Slow and steady wins the long race.

Be the Tortoise, Not the Hare

We live in an instant-gratification society. For instance, as an Amazon Prime member, you can order just about anything and have it delivered the next day. On social media, you can post your every thought and action and receive instant likes and comments. Everyone is reachable 24-7 by phone. But some things, like your professional life, don't work that way and never will. Building a career or a business is a marathon, not a sprint. It can take years—even decades—to establish yourself, your reputation, your brand, and expecting to be an overnight sensation will only lead to the frustration that results from false expectations. Slow and steady wins the long race. Take your time to develop the skills you need. No one expects you to know everything out of the gate.

Even the slowest tortoise can defeat the quickest hare, and even the proudest hare can learn a timeless lesson from the humblest tortoise: slow and steady wins the long race.

With automation comes progress but also anxiety.

Pick a Career That's Going to Age Well

Our world is changing at a dizzying pace. Things are happening so quickly, the technology lifespan for things like software, apps, iPhones, tablets, and computers is one to three years at best. The same is true of careers. With automation touching almost every industry, workers are increasingly competing with computers and robots instead of people. With automation comes progress but also anxiety. The workers whose jobs are being replaced wonder, *what should I do now? How can I earn a living? Do I have to start all over again?* It's a huge worry for many Americans. They see their worth diminishing. They know that technology can replace them. It's humbling and also very scary.

As I was choosing my career out of college, one of my major considerations was: what job is going to age well? If my dad were still alive, his line of work wouldn't have aged as well in an increasingly technologically driven era. He would have had to reinvent the way he did business in many ways. I have no doubt he would have been able to deal with the new landscape, but these changes can be frightening for many people. Taking a shot in your twenties is not a big deal, but it's a whole different thing when and you're established, you have a reputation, and you have to start over at fifty.

What careers will age well? The ones that are difficult or impossible to automate with our current technology. Hands-on professions like medical, dental, massage therapy, physical therapy, and senior care will likely never disappear. Our bodies will always need hands-on care. Skilled trades are another area that's here to stay—plumbers, carpenters, and electricians to fix things that go wrong in our homes and businesses. Even with the advent of online education, teachers will also have job security, especially those who work with children. Software developers and engineers will continue to be in high demand for the foreseeable future, as will accountants, attorneys, financial professionals, and entrepreneurs. Many jobs in the service industry will also stick around for a while, but these tend to be low-paying gig economy jobs with no benefits, so they may not be ideal for building a life.

Start Your Business on the Side

Let's say you've always dreamed of turning your hobby into a business, but you don't have the startup capital. Your hobby is baking healthy, delicious energy treats, and you believe you can grow it into a viable business, especially marketing your product to endurance athletes. The best approach is to keep your day job and start your business on the side. That way, you'll have guaranteed income and the resources to devote to putting together a business plan, perfecting your product, and thinking about branding, positioning, and marketing. You may want to look for investors or just go it alone in the beginning. You can scale your business gradually and effectively. And since, according to Forbes, 90 percent of startups fail, you'll have your backup plan if your venture doesn't succeed. You won't be desperately digging yourself out of a hole with nowhere to turn, a failed startup, and no job prospects. In other words, don't put all your eggs in one basket.

What If You Have No Idea What You Want to Pursue?

If you have no idea what you'd like to pursue, consider starting with a self-assessment. From there, you can match your values, aptitudes, skills, and interests with suitable professions. This assessment comes from the Indeed Guide: How to Choose a Career.

Self-assessment questions to consider:

1. What are your key values?
Example answers: Financial security, freedom, independence, giving back to society

2. What are your soft skills?
Example answers: Time management, communication, confidence, problem-solving, creativity

3. What are your technical skills?
Example answers: Data analytics, planning, research, languages, photography

4. What are your natural aptitudes?
Example answers: Writing, math, leadership, selling, project management, communicating, planning, technical problem-solving

5. What's your personality type?
Example answers: Myers-Briggs (MBTI) personality type, quiet, outgoing, confident, aggressive, loyal

6. What are your interests?
Example answers: Technology, writing, science, social work, medicine, design

Blindly doing what you love and hoping the money will follow is likely to have an unhappy ending unless you're one of the very lucky ones. By incorporating sound career advice, doing what you love doesn't have to leave you broke or drive you crazy. If you strategically pursue your passions, you won't end up killing them. And when you design your life around what you love *and* your need to earn a living, you can lead a rewarding life in which you feed your body and your soul.

CHAPTER 9

IF YOU CAN'T CONTROL WHAT YOU MAKE, CONTROL WHAT YOU SAVE AND SPEND

"Expect the best. Prepare for the worst. Capitalize on what comes." –Zig Ziglar

What is as important to our survival as food, water, oxygen, and shelter? I'll give you a hint: it's green and doesn't grow on trees. Yes, you guessed it—money. Much has been said about money not buying happiness. It's true. Money doesn't buy happiness, but happiness is hard to achieve without money. Generating enough money to live a comfortable life is a marathon, not a sprint. In other words, you must generate sufficient income to more than cover your expenses over your adult lifespan, which could be up to six or seven decades! Remember, you might have to finance the last two or three decades without income and with increased health care and housing costs.

If you don't create a plan, you'll be a victim of your circumstances, and it could be a bumpy ride. Without a plan, you'll run the risk of having to start over again and again. You may have to restart repeatedly—with less energy as you age and less time as your responsibilities increase. Remember that everyone has an expiration date! The plan is a simple equation:

Generating Income + Wise Spending + Saving + Investing = Financial Well-Being

Generating Income

Let's look at the first part of the equation: Generating Income. Most of us have to work or start a business to generate income. Work doesn't have to be a four-letter word if you choose carefully. How can you do this? Ask: *What means the world to me? What makes me smile? What gets my heart pumping?* Then figure out a way to make it pay. If you're struggling too much, it will detract from your love of work.

This requires knowing what you're good at, what you enjoy, and which professions will enable you to earn a decent living. Your work doesn't have to be your ultimate life's passion, but it should be something that makes you feel you're using your natural gifts and that adds to the quality of your life. Then, once you've chosen a career path, settle in for the long haul. Know that it's going to take persistent hard work to earn enough to buy a car, house, and health care, support a family, and set yourself up for retirement. If you're doing what you enjoy and applying your talents, working hard can be extremely satisfying and rewarding—intrinsically and financially.

What About Pursuing My Dreams?

Not everyone is lucky enough to make a living doing what they love, but it is definitely possible with talent, persistence, and luck. If what you love is in high demand, you are one of the fortunate ones. Let's say you love accounting, spreadsheets, and crunching numbers. Thankfully for you, accounting is a profession that is in high demand and rewards skilled people handsomely. There's no need for a backup plan.

Let's take another example—someone who would like to sing and perform professionally. This path is more difficult in that musicians are often underpaid, and steady gigs can be hard to come by. So, as an aspiring musician, it is wise to have a backup plan—a profession that is in higher demand, such as computer programming. By all means, go for it as a professional musician to test the waters, but if you find it is too difficult to make ends meet, you may have to go to your backup plan and do your music on the side. This is just the reality of the marketplace—too many musicians chasing too few dollars. It doesn't mean you have to give up your dream; it just means that you will tweak it a little bit so you can make a living.

Spending Wisely

There's a simple approach to deciding how best to spend your hard-earned money—simply ask why. *Why am I spending this money?* When you answer, you must be brutally honest with yourself. Then apply the need-to-have versus the nice-to-have standard. If your answer is: because it makes me truly happy, because it makes me healthier, or because I'm building my future, then your spending is probably justified.

But, on the other hand, if it's just a nice-to-have expenditure, then you don't need to spend the money. If you ask yourself, why am

I spending this money? and your answer is "everyone else does it," "it's trendy," "it seems like the thing to do," or "I want to impress others," you will want to take a serious look at your spending.

Playing the Long Game

As with building personal relationships and achieving job satisfaction, managing your money well and saving for retirement isn't likely to give you instant gratification. Why? Because you're not going to tap into that money for decades—maybe thirty or forty years. For many, this trade-off can be difficult. It can be tempting to spend money now on things that give you a temporary mood boost, like a new car, clothes, digital devices, fancy dinners, and lavish trips, to name a few luxury items.

Everything in our society prompts us to buy newer, bigger, better, shinier things. That's what keeps business humming. For instance, even though we might have an old smartphone that does the trick, we are barraged by marketing and advertising messages dangling the new, fancy features of the latest smartphone. The company would have us believe that we absolutely can't live without the latest and greatest phone. It can be a challenge to step back from these messages and ask: "Do I really need to spend $1,200 on a new smartphone?" It can be especially tempting if everyone around us has taken the bait and is showing off the new bells and whistles. When such temptations arise, it's good to remind yourself that you're playing the long game—of saving, investing, and wisely spending your hard-earned money. Apply the strategy of asking yourself, "why do I need a new smartphone?" If your answer is, "because my friends have one," "because I care what my friends think," or "because it has cool new features," you probably don't need one. If your answer is, "I need it to build my business" or "I need it for my job," it may be a justified expense. Then it is an investment in your future.

It's difficult to be passionate about saving when you're not going to be instantly gratified—you're not going to see, feel, or touch the money for at least 30 years.

Saving and Investing Aren't Sexy

It's true that saving and investing aren't sexy. Why? Because saving and investing are slow, incremental activities that require endurance, patience, and going the distance. It's not heart-pounding, fast-paced wheeling, dealing, and day-trading that may generate quick returns. It's more like the drip-drip-drip of a faucet that fills up a bucket, slowly but surely, over several weeks. Or, to put it another way—you can't lose a hundred pounds in a day, so why would you expect your stocks to double overnight? Waiting for results can try the patience of even the most persevering people.

One of the first times Jeff Bezos met Warren Buffett, he approached Buffett and said, "Your investment strategy is so common sense and simple. I wonder why everyone doesn't do it. You're one of the wealthiest men in the world."

Warren said, "Jeff, that's smart of you to say, and I appreciate it. The reason is no one wants to get rich slowly." Warren Buffett, by owning blue-chip, dividend-paying stocks, and holding them for a long time, achieves long-term gains instead of short-term gains—and is worth billions of dollars.

That has always stuck with me.

It takes emotional intelligence to be a savvy investor and to be disciplined in saving. It's difficult to be passionate about saving when you're not going to see, feel, touch the money for thirty years. In other words, gratification is delayed by at least three decades. In a world of temptations and status comparisons, it takes serious willpower to say no to things that will make us seem more beautiful, impressive, popular, and sought-after than the next person. But appearances can be deceiving. People who appear to be the wealthiest actually may not be. In fact, they could be wearing or driving their bank accounts rather than building robust savings. The truth is, they're spending to impress instead of spending wisely and saving for their future.

Build a rainy-day fund by automatically investing money from each paycheck.

Rainy-Day Fund

Especially when we're young, we may not see the need for a rainy-day fund. But given that life is unpredictable, and we don't know what's in the cards for our health and well-being, a rainy-day fund is absolutely essential to get through the rough times. How can you do this? By investing in the background—taking money from each paycheck and automatically investing it, so you always have a rainy-day fund and a healthy retirement. It's especially important now because, in less than twenty years, Social Security may be a watered-down version of its former self.

Let's look at an example that illustrates the importance of having a rainy-day fund. Samantha has been married for ten years and doesn't earn enough to support herself. She relies on her husband's income to survive. Her husband leaves her unexpectedly and then loses his job, so he can't pay alimony. Meanwhile, Samantha scrambles to afford the basics—rent, utilities, and health care. Every month she has a shortfall and racks up credit card debt. If she had a rainy-day fund, it would have helped her survive while she set up a new life for herself. Without a rainy-day fund, she's buried in credit card debt and has to start her new life by digging herself out of a hole.

I always say money can't buy happiness, but it can buy choices, and choices can lead to lower stress. This, in turn, allows you to better prioritize your life and focus on the things that make you happy. I chose my profession—financial advising—for this very reason. When I lost my father, I said to myself: *Mom is scared; she doesn't know exactly what to do financially, and I have no answers for her.* I started thinking about how I might help her. Along with the many other rewards, going into financial advising has allowed me to have answers for her. My mom always tells me how happy she is that she can call me, and I'll have the answer. I don't know if she realizes it, but that's why I chose what I do. I think it worked.

Just like I do with my mom, my goal is to give my clients as many choices as are humanly possible. I like to make a fundamental, positive change in peoples' lives. I am not creating happiness for them. I am simply giving them the option to choose what they want to do in life, where they want to travel, how they want to educate their children, and how they want to retire. And options help people feel that they have the freedom and means to live their best life.

Managing your money well is a critically important piece in leaving a smile on your face at the end of the day. It isn't about acquiring material possessions. It's about not being wracked with anxiety about not having enough money or having a crisis that could bankrupt you. It's about having a plan in which you earn money doing something you love, spend wisely, and save and invest. It's about feeling comfortable with your financial situation—one that sets you up for a life well-lived, which is a huge part of the happiness equation.

CHAPTER 10

ACHIEVING WORK-LIFE BALANCE

"Vision without action is merely a dream." –Joel Barker

Living the life of your dreams doesn't just magically happen; it is something that requires envisioning, planning, and executing. From the outside, it may appear that people living their dreams are very lucky, but the truth is, they likely created a blueprint for their success and carried it out. In other words, they knew where they wanted to go and worked hard, day in and day out, to achieve their dreams. They were also not workaholics or playaholics but people who struck a balance by incorporating work and play, relationships, and passions. Work + play + relationships + passions = balanced success.

Setting the Scope of Your Daily Vision

You may be thinking: is it really necessary to have a vision for each day? Yes, it is, and here's why and how. View your goals as the summit of a mountain you are setting out to climb. Each day is like a stepping-stone toward that summit. The best way to take on each day is to identify your top three tasks for a given day. You might have many more things to do, but focusing on the top three will help you prioritize and keep you from becoming overwhelmed. Being overwhelmed can affect your productivity in that you might become avoidant or despondent, with a cascade of things on your to-do list. Once you've completed your top three tasks, you can move on to the next priorities. But in a worst-case scenario, if you only complete your top three, you'll have had a productive day.

Time Blocking

If you don't schedule it, it probably won't happen. Time blocking is the act of scheduling everything in your day, including meals, work projects, and other activities in order to better manage your time and discover where hours are being wasted or underutilized. Time blocking is the practice of planning out every minute of your day in advance and dedicating specific time blocks for given tasks and responsibilities.

By scheduling every minute of your day, you protect yourself from distractions and sharpen your focus. Also, contrary to popular belief about multitasking enhancing your productivity, single-tasking—focusing on one task at a time—can make you up to 80 percent more productive than splitting your attention across multiple tasks. For example, let's say you have a business proposal due in a couple of days. Throughout the workday, you check email a few times every hour. Each time you shift your focus to email and go down the rabbit hole of responding, you splinter your focus. You may not realize it, but every time you pull your focus away from your proposal, it takes time and energy to remember where you were and ramp up again.

So, time blocking to check your emails—perhaps once or twice a day—will greatly improve your productivity. This will allow you to be laser-focused on your proposal and complete it much more efficiently than if you had let emails distract you.

According to *Deep Work* author Cal Newport, "People ask why I bother with such a detailed level of planning. My answer is simple: it generates a massive amount of productivity. A forty-hour time-blocked workweek, I estimate, produces the same amount of output as a sixty-plus hour work week pursued without structure."

Achieving Work-Life Balance

Notice that the time-blocking section included setting aside time for life and play. All work and no play make for a life of drudgery, unless you're one of the rare people for whom work is your play. The fact is that working too much can have dramatic negative consequences. Working in excess of fifty-five hours a week raises the risk of heart attack, stroke, depression, anxiety and insomnia. And to add insult to injury, long hours don't even increase performance. Also, according to the *Harvard Business Review*, studies show that IQ drops thirteen points when workers are in a state of tunnel-vision busyness (being so busy that we can only focus on what's right in front of us).

So, what is work-life balance, and how can you achieve it? Let go of perfection in achieving work-life balance; prioritize your health, self-care, and time off; and unplug from your digital devices and set boundaries.

- **Accept that there's no work-life nirvana.** When you imagine work-life balance, you may envision yourself going to work at 8:00 a.m. and signing off at 5:00 p.m. Once home, you exercise with your family—perhaps you take a family bike ride, make a homemade meal, put the kids to bed, and then spend time on your favorite hobby before bed. The truth is you might get home and find that the kids have homework demands that make it impossible to exercise then. Your mother calls with an emergency you must attend to. You run out of time for a homemade meal and have to order takeout; finally, you collapse into bed with no time for your hobby. Feeling bad about not striking your ideal work-life balance that day will only add insult to injury. Accept that on some days, your work-life balance will just be getting through the day and dropping into bed for some much-needed rest. That's OK. It's called real life.

• **Put your health first.** Let's face it: if you don't have your health, you have nothing. Too many people fail to prioritize health until it's too late. Perhaps they didn't put their health first until they were diagnosed with a chronic or a terminal health condition. Now, they're faced with managing their health condition instead of preventing it. Don't wait to make sure your lifestyle promotes physical and mental health and wellness. Perhaps you're too busy with your family to exercise when you get home from work. Set aside your lunch hour to exercise and then eat lunch at your desk.

• **Take vacations.** Americans don't typically use all their vacation time, which, incidentally, is among the lowest allotted to workers in the developed world. One study found that 55 percent of Americans did not use all of their paid vacation time. Yet an annual vacation can cut heart attack risk in half. Among middle-aged men at high risk of coronary heart disease, those who take frequent annual vacations cut their chances of dying from coronary heart disease by a whopping one-third. Blood pressure, heart rate, and stress levels are reduced even by taking a short holiday of one to three days. Don't feel guilty about taking your vacation time. It's there for a reason—to give you much-needed rest and relaxation, which will actually make you more productive in the long run.

- **Unplug from your devices.** The downside of having devices that make you accessible around the clock is that your boss and coworkers can reach you and make demands 24-7. Make a habit of unplugging when you're away from work, and let your boss and colleagues know you're not reachable. Otherwise, they'll get into the bad habit of interrupting your life. Anyone can be trained, your boss and colleagues included.

Being Mindful of Time Wasters

How many times have you taken a break from work to check out Facebook or Instagram, and you end up spending thirty minutes lurking, liking, and commenting? You promised yourself you would take just a short break and get back to work. But the lure of friends' posts sucked you in and kept you there. Facebook and Instagram are two of the many modern time sucks, many of which include unproductive screen time. If you're not careful, you'll wake up decades later and think, how did I get here and where did all my time go?

The key here is to be conscious about time-wasters. If you love to grab your phone or computer and engage with your friends on social media, carve out time to do that. So, if you want to check in with friends on Facebook or Instagram, put a time limit on it. You could even set an alarm for twenty minutes. And stick to it! Unless you're using Facebook and Instagram to launch and promote your business, there's nothing on either that supports your vision.

———

"The more you are focused on time—past and future—the more you miss the now, the most precious thing there is."
–Eckhart Tolle

———

Another example of a time-waster is jumping on YouTube for what is initially a quick hit. But it takes you down a path of watching video after video, and before you know it, you've wasted hours YouTubing. If this brings you joy and satisfaction, by all means, be a YouTuber, but block off time to do so, and be conscious of the time you spend on your pastime. Be aware of your tendencies and cut them off at the pass when you have other things to accomplish. Perhaps limit yourself to an hour a week and stick to it. By restricting your usage, you'll appreciate your YouTubing so much more—and you won't feel guilt or regret over time wasted.

Staying Present
Scores of books and articles have been written about staying present—being in the now. But so many of us find it difficult to do. Why? Because we're either dwelling on the past or obsessing over the future. Perhaps you have regrets about the past and hopes or

expectations for the future. Perhaps you are anticipating something you have planned for the future. The surest path to discontentment is living anywhere but in the present. Because the present is all we have. The past is behind us, and the future is yet to arrive. Of course, we can and should plan for the future, but living there only causes anxiety and detracts from the present. View the present as a gift. The more we can be where we are—right here and now—the happier we'll be. You won't feel the deep regret of things that didn't happen in the past or anticipatory anxiety over things that may or may not happen in the future. Practicing gratitude for what you have in your life right now will greatly amplify your happiness.

Watching for Signs of Burnout

Have you ever hit a wall at work that, no matter what you tried, you couldn't get past? You felt unfocused, depleted, uninspired, and you were operating at less than 50 percent capacity. It is likely that you were experiencing burnout. Job burnout is a state of physical and/or emotional exhaustion that includes a sense of reduced accomplishment and loss of personal identity. If you suspect that you might be burned out, review this checklist from the Mayo Clinic. If you answer "yes" to a majority of the questions, you are likely experiencing burnout.

- Have you become cynical or critical at work?
- Do you drag yourself to work and have trouble getting started?
- Have you become irritable or impatient with co-workers, customers or clients?
- Do you lack the energy to be consistently productive?
- Do you find it hard to concentrate?

- Do you lack satisfaction from your achievements?
- Do you feel disillusioned about your job?
- Are you using food, drugs or alcohol to feel better or to simply not feel?
- Have your sleep habits changed?
- Are you troubled by unexplained headaches, stomach or bowel problems, or other physical complaints?

The way to deal with burnout is to incorporate the strategies in the work/life balance section. You may also want to work with your boss to scale back some responsibilities, even if it's temporary. Make sure you take frequent breaks from work, such as getting up and walking outside for ten minutes while listening to music or your favorite podcast. Also, cut back on your to-do list so that it includes only essential items, as opposed to nice-to-haves. A to-do list with too many tasks can by itself stress you out and be paralyzing. If your burnout is extreme and affecting your mental and physical health, see a therapist to help you structure your life for optimal performance and well-being.

Designing your life to balance work and play can be a tricky proposition. If you're too focused on work, you might drive yourself to burnout and short-change your dreams. If you're too focused on play, you could be missing out on work satisfaction and failing to achieve professional and financial well-being. If your focus is on balance, incorporating work and play, relationships, family, and passions, and you design your life accordingly, you are more likely to lead the life of your dreams.

CHAPTER 11

CONSCIOUSNESS IS THE
ULTIMATE DRUG

———

"Five percent of the people think; 10 percent of the people think they think; and the other 85 percent would rather die than think." –Thomas Edison

———

Addiction in America has reached crisis proportions. According to the National Survey on Drug Use and Health, 20.4 million American adults battled a substance use disorder in 2018. That same year, 2.4 million people—or nearly one out of every eight adults with a substance use disorder—simultaneously struggled with both alcohol and drug use disorders. Since 1990, drug overdose deaths have more than tripled. And if drug and alcohol addictions aren't enough, a newly emerging addiction is sweeping the country—excessive use of social media, gaming, and gambling are destroying millions of lives as well.

There are many theories about why Americans are so addicted, reaching for drugs, alcohol, and digital devices to alter their moods.

Reasons include to quell anxiety, curb depression, alleviate stress, numb feelings, and cope with the stressors of modern-day living. A predominant theory claims Americans are desperately seeking a dopamine boost—a chemical that affects the brain's pleasure and reward centers. Other theories maintain that pharmaceutical companies and doctors are all too willing to promote and push prescription drugs on Americans upon the mention of the slightest pain or discomfort. And finally, some point to the instant-gratification culture in the United States. There's always something to reach for to fill the void. Instead of sitting with the discomfort inherent in life, many prefer to reach for a quick fix.

While substances may provide temporary relief, the truth is that cultivating consciousness without mood-altering substances or distractions may be the ultimate drug. It can open your eyes and expand your mind in ways that transform your life. The thought of cultivating natural awareness without mood-altering substances can be truly hair-raising for people, especially if they have been relying on a substance to do the heavy lifting of life.

Not only are Americans highly addicted, but they are also unaccustomed to the quiet contemplation of being. Our culture is so focused on compulsive doing and consumption that being is lost in the shuffle. Busyness is the way we demonstrate to the world how successful and important we are. Typically, when you ask someone how they are, they say, "Oh, I'm so busy!" When was the last time you asked a friend or acquaintance how they were, and they said, "I'm enjoying just being?" Unless you were at an ashram or a yoga retreat, probably never—right? Nonstop activity leaves us frazzled, harried, and burned out, reaching for substances to alleviate our anguish.

Cultivating Consciousness

What is consciousness, exactly? It's the state of being awake and aware of one's thoughts, emotions, and actions. Cultivating consciousness is another way of saying, be more aware of how you move through the world and react to people and experiences. This isn't saying you need to be sober for the rest of your life. As many of us know, moderation is the real key. It's more of an observatory standpoint and a want/need to ask "why."

You may be convinced that cultivating consciousness is the way to go, but where do you even start? First, you must realize that in the beginning, you'll likely experience some discomfort as you unplug from perpetual doing. You might feel antsy and anxious because you're daring to step off the frantic treadmill of American life. Be prepared to tolerate some discomfort as you slow your mind and body. Also, it will take discipline and commitment to cultivate consciousness. Some of the recommended approaches may feel boring, slow, and tedious. Just know that this is completely normal. Getting off the frenzied pace is like overcoming any addiction. Discomfort is part of the healing process.

To start cultivating your consciousness, try one or more of these activities: meditate, journal, practice introspection, talk less and listen more, pursue lifelong learning, and wander and wonder.

Meditate to Quiet the Chatter

Meditation seems to be the advice for every ailment these days. Feeling stressed? Meditate. Burned out? Meditate. Relationship troubles? Meditate. For some people the idea of sitting still, repeating a mantra, focusing on in-breaths and out-breaths, and staring into space sounds like cruel and unusual torture.

We all live in our own little universes, barraged by thoughts and feelings. I'm sure you've noticed your mind chatter, like having a play-by-play sports anchor in your head providing commentary on your life—the good, the bad, and the ugly. And sometimes this voice is relentlessly critical, holding you to impossible standards. Wouldn't it be nice if the sports anchor in your mind were on your side—like the very best coach you've ever had? Doing nothing in silence and stillness in our lively, action-oriented culture may be just the antidote, but is it worth the effort? Yes. It helps you live in the present. It quiets the chatter. It harnesses your mind, so your thoughts work for and not against you. Or, if negative thoughts do arise, you just watch them come and go, detached from the outcome.

Scientists haven't yet identified the true nature of consciousness, but many agree that it can be measured by observing your brainwave patterns. Theta and delta brainwaves become more prominent as you go deeper into meditation. Delta brainwaves are slow, low frequency, and deeply penetrating, occurring in deep meditation and dreamless sleep. Theta brainwaves occur most often in sleep but are also present in deep meditation. Theta is the gateway to learning, memory, and intuition. Meditation triggers inspirational flashes of creativity, allowing you to access old memories and enabling lucid dreaming.

To begin, you may want to work with a meditation instructor, participate in a structured meditation, or use a meditation application. You can also follow these easy instructions:

1. Sit or lie comfortably. You may want to buy a meditation chair or cushion.

2. Close your eyes or softly direct your gaze downward.

3. Don't control your breath; simply breathe naturally.

4. Focus your attention on your breath and on how your body moves with each inhalation and exhalation.

Journal for Self-discovery

Journaling is an easily accessible tool for self-discovery. It allows you to express your regrets and worries on the page and tune into the present moment. As you write in your journal, you focus your mind and engage with your innermost thoughts and feelings, bringing things to light that you weren't previously aware of. You may sometimes wonder, *what's the use? My journal is filled with bitching and moaning.* That's OK. Once you commit your grievances to the page, you'll find that they're less burdensome, or they may even vanish. It's an opportunity to communicate with the subconscious feelings you might be ignoring. The act of writing provides a forum for those feelings so you can more easily shine light on them. Here's how to start the habit.

1. Buy a journal and a writing utensil that inspire you so that you'll be more likely to journal.

2. Write as though no one is watching. Because it's true; no one will ever read your journal without your consent.

3. Don't worry about grammar, spelling, or punctuation. Free your hand to write what's in your mind and heart. Remember: this is for you only.

4. If you experience writer's block, start with some questions: What am I feeling? What am I thinking? What's on my mind?

What bothered me today? What inspired me today? Or come up with your own writing prompts.

———

"Why" questions trap us in our past; "what" questions help us create a better future." –Tasha Eurich

———

Practice Introspection

Introspection is another great approach for cultivating consciousness. It is defined as the examination or observation of one's own mental and emotional processes. Some have dubbed introspection "navel-gazing," implying that it is excessive, self-involved, and unnecessary. Of course, everything can be taken to an extreme, and introspection, when not balanced with action, can backfire, resulting in someone being overly self-involved. We've all encountered self-absorbed people who process their thoughts and feelings ad nauseam; they're stuck in an endless feedback loop of unproductive self-reflection.

When you strike the right balance between introspection and living, time spent alone in contemplation will be positive—a rich environment for personal growth and creativity. It will be a process of healthy self-reflection, examination, and exploration, which boosts your mental health.

According to organizational psychologist Tasha Eurich, the problem with introspection is that we don't always do it right. When we're struggling to understand, we often ask "Why" questions, such as "Why did that happen to me?" "Why did I do that?" "Why did my spouse leave?" or "Why is my life so hard?"

But "why" questions can be impossible to answer; they summon act-of-God responses. And thus, they can keep us stuck in a victim mentality, with conclusions like "life isn't fair." "Why" questions can keep us ruminating because there's really nowhere to go; instead, we just go around and around, chasing our tail. On the other hand, "what" questions help us craft a better future. "What" questions cultivate self-awareness, promote understanding, and prompt empowering responses. For example, "What's going on with me?" "What am I feeling?" "What messages am I telling myself?" "What's another perspective?" or "What can I do to respond better?"

Eurich writes, "When it comes to developing internal self-awareness, I like to use a simple tool that I call *What Not Why*. *Why* questions can draw us to our limitations; *what* questions help us see our potential. *Why* questions stir up negative emotions; *what* questions keep us curious. *Why* questions trap us in our past; *what* questions help us create a better future."

Talk Less and Listen More

The United States is a very talkative culture, so much so that listening increasingly seems like a lost art. When's the last time you felt someone really listened to you? I'm not talking about those times the listener was tuning in while waiting for their turn to talk but rather when they genuinely tuned into your message, ideas, emotions, and state of mind. It has probably been a while since someone deeply listened to you—right? Even though talking seems more highly valued than listening in our culture, listening can actually teach you more. Listening not only provides insights into your conversation partner but into your way of being, thinking, and living. It may seem counterintuitive, but listening to others can help you learn about yourself.

If you tend to be overly talkative when interacting with friends, family, and colleagues, challenge yourself to sit back and listen more often—really listen. I struggle to do this myself at times. Use the following questions as your guide to deepen your ability to listen to others. You will be amazed by what you learn about others and yourself when you're not cueing up your next talking point, argument, or point of view.

- What are they trying to convey?
- What are they feeling?
- What is their state of mind?
- What do they need right now?
- What subtle messages are encoded in their communication?
- What is their body language revealing?

"He not busy being born is busy dying." –**Bob Dylan**

Become a Lifelong Learner

Once you're officially done with school—whether it's high school, college, or graduate school—become a lifelong learner. Stay curious; stay hungry. Live with your eyes wide open, looking for opportunities to stretch yourself. Don't get too comfortable or complacent with your daily routine; otherwise, you will stop learning and growing. Put yourself in uncomfortable situations and try things you've never tried before. Seek new experiences and block them into your schedule.

"Not all who wander are lost." –J. R. R. Tolkien

Take Time to Wander and Wonder

J. R. R. Tolkien, author of *The Lord of the Rings,* wrote, "Not all who wander are lost." In fact, some might argue that you must wander to find yourself. Why? Wandering is a sacred time when goal-oriented behavior is suspended. It's the in-between time when you can explore and learn things about yourself and the world that you wouldn't have likely discovered if you were sticking to an agenda. Wandering allows for serendipity and magic.

For example, after Hannah completed law school and passed the bar, she decided to take a road trip out West. After seeing the country and the beautiful landscape, she was motivated to go into environmental law. She ended up working for the National Resources Defense Council (NRDC). Imagine if Hannah hadn't wandered; she never would have found her life's work.

Travel to learn how other people live. If that's not feasible, tap into other resources to explore. Watch documentaries and read nonfiction accounts written by people from other countries and cultures. Live vicariously through friends and acquaintances who've traveled to places you haven't visited. This is not about posing for selfies by the Eiffel Tower or the Great Wall of China, even though that can be fun; it's about learning about other countries' history, cultural paradigms, standards of success, happiness, beauty, and well-being.

Wondering is to the mind as wandering is to the body. Wondering is setting your mind free to daydream, to be untethered to to-do lists, tasks, and obligations; it can promote creativity and innovation. It can also lead to self-inquiry and meaning-making. In other words, by letting your mind roam, you can happen upon ideas and insights that spur you to try new things that not only enrich your life but have the potential to blow your life wide open. So, next time you notice you're daydreaming, let your mind soar instead of bringing it back to the task at hand. Your work can wait, but your life can't.

Cultivating consciousness without mood-altering substances or distractions may be the best, cheapest high around. To get there, though, you must learn to take reality head-on. Thankfully, there are easy-to-use approaches, including meditation, journaling, practicing introspection, talking less and listening more, pursuing lifelong learning, and wandering and wondering. Try all these approaches, or mix and match, and watch your consciousness expand. The sky's the limit!

CHAPTER 12

MAKING EMOTIONS YOUR ALLY

———

"Our deepest fear is not that we are inadequate. Our deepest fear is that we are powerful beyond measure. It is our light, not our darkness, that most frightens us. We ask ourselves who am I to be brilliant, gorgeous, talented? Actually, who are you not to be? Your playing small does not serve the world. There is nothing enlightened about shrinking so that others won't feel insecure around you. We are all meant to shine, as children do. ... As we let our own light shine, we unconsciously give other people permission to do the same. As we are liberated from our own fear, our presence automatically liberates others."
–Marianne Williamson

———

Everyone has heard the expression: you're your own worst enemy. And it's true. I've seen it with my own eyes. I've known people who are filled with self-loathing and thus sabotage everything they do. They get hung out to dry by their own emotions. When they have a strong emotional response to something, they get trapped in a web of feeling instead of cutting through the noise and staying on track with their lives. Perhaps they are going through a breakup and dwell on it for the better part of six months. That's time they'll never get back. The truth is: they're the only ones who can save themselves, and if they wait for others to swoop in to save the day, they'll be waiting a long time.

Self-loathing is one of the biggest mistakes a person can make. Feeling bad for yourself is the key to failure in life. Because the truth is, as captured in a quote from the movie *A Bronx Tale*, nobody cares. Just two simple words capture such a powerful universal truth. Nobody cares, fundamentally. You could build masterpieces, wildly successful companies, or even empires. Or you could do nothing with your life. Once you die, it's over. Win, lose, or draw; nobody cares. A fundamental, unforgiving, hard truth that few people realize is that nobody, in the grand scheme of things, cares about you like you. Nobody cares about your life and what happens to you like you do. No one ever will. Nobody will care about your happiness and your achieving a healthy mind and body as much as you. You are alone on an island with that eternal truth. Many people never come to this realization in their lives; they keep it at arm's length. But the sooner you can accept it, the better. Everyone gets dealt a shit hand at some point in their life—in fact, at many points in their lives. So, you must be prepared and know what you're going to do with your cards. You might not know exactly what to do, but you should be ready to play a hand. You can't just sit there and fold.

If you discover you're feeling bad for yourself, remember that you care more than anyone about you. You must have your own back and push yourself out the door, propel yourself beyond your comfort zone, and go for your dreams, keeping in mind that dreams are made of steady, solid hard work every day. Some call it the grind, but I call it a daily opportunity to manifest your dream life.

Emotions Are Pointless

When we experience intense emotions, blood recedes from the thinking part of the brain, the cerebral cortex, and rushes to its oldest and most involuntary part, the "reptilian" stem, crippling the intake of new information. In effect, you're disabling your ability to think rationally.

Whether you're feeling rage, anger, excitement, disgust, horror, or joy, trying to act rationally just delays whatever you're going to do after you feel that emotion. Emotion is the unnecessary drama that precedes the action. So, if something negative happens, I don't react. I try to understand the context of what is happening, cut through the emotion, set it aside, and then do whatever needs to be done. The emotion just delays the doing.

You shouldn't let emotions steer you. Emotions are fleeting, like the weather. Just as a storm might blow in, churn things up, and blow out, your emotions can churn up your insides and send you reeling. Wouldn't you prefer to do without the internal tornado?

Social media is a prime example of the fleeting nature of emotions. When someone likes your Instagram post, good feelings wash over you. While you may welcome the affirmation, it's fleeting and steering you in the wrong direction. It's distracting and pulling you into a world filled with false rewards and empty promises. So rather than riding the waves of social media-driven rewards, identify and document your true focus and associated goals and outcomes. Set your sights on achieving that, and sideline your emotions, because they will lead you astray. Know what you want to do and do it.

At the end of the day, my inner fire and thoughts are focused on the things I have prioritized and my endgame. I don't want to complicate things with emotions; my internal compass is already pointed in the right direction. I know where I'm going, and emotion throws me off-course every time.

The Problem of Sticky Emotions

When emotions become a persistent problem that interferes with your daily functioning, and you can't set them aside, no matter how hard you try, it's time for some self-examination or even therapy. Let's say you have difficulty controlling your anxiety in your everyday life. It is very likely your anxiety stems from childhood trauma. Trauma doesn't have to be extreme, like child abuse; it can be as commonplace as your parents divorcing. Perhaps one of your parents moved away, and you only saw that parent once or twice a year. That's a major loss—almost like the death of a parent. If left unresolved, it is likely this issue will dog you as an adult. Perhaps you find that you have anxiety anytime a friend or loved one seems to be distancing themself from you. This is likely connected to your childhood trauma. Resolving these early issues should lessen your anxiety, and help you have a more rational emotional response to things that happen in adulthood.

It's about healing the child inside you. If you think about it, when we look at ourselves in the mirror, we just see a kid who got older. Inside each of us is the child we always were. Children are innately scientists. They approach a rock and lift it up to discover what's underneath. Maybe they find a worm or a roly-poly. The kid inside of us is just a person who sees the world but doesn't judge. All kids are trying to do is smile, but at some point, we lose that kid. Maybe it's too much hardship; maybe we had to be too serious for too long.

What's the crossover point where you go from being the kid—alive and spontaneous—to constrained and serious? When does the switch happen? And does it signal a point of no return? Who was that person? Why can't we access them anymore? It becomes harder to see the big picture. You might get lost and launch an unnecessary journey of self-discovery instead of simply identifying your emotional needs.

Focus on Genuine Emotions

Another approach to managing emotions is knowing yourself well enough to focus only on the genuine emotions. Find out what makes you tick by asking, every time you find yourself having a strong reaction, *why am I having this reaction? What is the rational reason behind it?* If you allow yourself to be honest, you quickly realize there is a common denominator from which all your emotions derive.

———

There is no such thing as good or bad emotions; emotions are simply data.

———

There is no such thing as good or bad emotions; emotions are simply data. Taking the step back from *I am angry* to *I feel angry* creates space and shrinks the emotion. Recognize that your emotions are providing valuable information about you and the world.

Here's a step-by-step approach that will help you manage your emotions:

1. Ask: *Why am I experiencing this right now?*

2. Identify the root cause.

3. Convert your emotions into rational thoughts.

4. Table your emotions.

5. Address the situation with concrete steps.

Digital Rollercoaster Ride

You log onto your social media account, and a friend has posted something offensive in response to your last post, which was meant to be innocuous. You fire back. Your friend doubles down. Your blood is boiling, and you write something in the heat of the moment. Your friend fires back. Other people weigh in. You're furious. And for what? An innocent social media post sent you through the roof for no good reason.

Another example: you read some very bad news, such as that half of Australia is burning in uncontrolled wildfires, and a billion animals have died. It makes you feel depressed and apocalyptic about the planet's future and your life. You start your day feeling helpless and pessimistic.

While it's fine to stay connected to others and informed about the world, it does you no good if it sends you into fits of rage or bouts of depression that color your mood and dampen your motivation. As I discussed earlier, social media and news are designed to keep you tuned in and addicted. The addictive design drives traffic, clicks, and viewership for ad revenue. You are just roadkill on the digital highway. You may want to temper the emotional roller-coaster ride that social media and news trigger and pace yourself on the consumption of both. It will even out your emotional state and give you more peace of mind, especially if you are easily triggered.

Expectations and Emotions

Expectations are a tricky business. Expecting life to turn out the way you want is guaranteed to disappoint because life doesn't work that way. Pinning hopes for happiness on unrealistic expectations will only lead to unhappiness. But if you can acknowledge your feelings when your expectations aren't met, and adjust your expectations, you will greatly lessen your anxiety.

Imagine you are stuck in traffic, running late for a meeting, and cursing at the traffic jam. You had left your home early, expecting to arrive at your destination twenty minutes ago, and you're still ten minutes away. You tell yourself, *I have to get there on time!* Then someone tries to merge in front of you, and you perceive the driver as out of line. Plus, he's going to make you even later. You frantically lay on your horn. Then you think, *I'm being ridiculous. It's not her fault. I'm worked up because I expected to arrive at my meeting on time and I am stuck in traffic—something I have no control over. Stuff happens. I'll get there as soon as I can.*

Surprisingly, this simple acknowledgment lifts your mood. By saying to yourself what you are feeling and letting go of your unrealistic expectations, you have lessened the power of your emotions and merged emotions and cognitions. Instead of admonishing yourself, you acknowledge the emotions, and in so doing make them your ally.

Expectations are only warranted if they are backed up by daily, habitual action. Some strategies for doing that include:

- Under-promising and over-performing.
- Holding yourself accountable and not handcuffing yourself to unrealistic expectations.
- Altering expectations to lessen anxiety.
- Showing up on time.
- Building in buffers for deadlines.

Emotions in Relationships

Emotions in relationships can be a powder keg on the verge of exploding if you're not careful. And it makes sense because with love and connection comes vulnerability. Why? Because a relationship is two different people with varying needs and wants, interpreting each other's behavior through your lenses. This inevitably leads to misinterpretations, which can escalate misunderstanding and lead to conflict and hurt. We say things we didn't mean to say that can inflict permanent damage.

When emotions are running high with a friend, a colleague, or a loved one, it's best to take a step back and try to see the world through their eyes. You're not denying yourself the right to your emotions; you're just taking a little break in order to see more clearly. Ask: *What factors are causing them to feel these emotions or think these thoughts?* Being able to detach and assess will enable you to remain in relative control of your relationships. In a way, most people are exacting control over others each time they interact. Indeed, there are some equitable outcomes, but most are trying to achieve given outcomes from each interaction. And to achieve outcomes, you must take a step back.

Don't Let Emotions Hijack You

It's important to remember that you are not your emotions. You have emotions, just like you have thoughts; they float in and out like clouds in the sky. If we let them, emotions have a way of hijacking us, blindfolding us, and taking us off-course—sometimes a great distance from where we want to be. We cannot always choose our emotions, but we can choose how we respond to them.

It pays to live the life of our dreams. And while emotions can be a temptress, pulling us into their evocative sway, it's best to stave off the temptation and walk the path we've envisioned for ourselves. For, as Marianne Williamson asks, what if we are powerful beyond measure, and the only thing limiting us is ourselves?

CHAPTER 13

THE PSYCHOLOGY OF HAPPINESS

"A wandering mind is an unhappy mind. The ability to think about what is not happening is a cognitive achievement that comes at an emotional cost." –Dan Gilbert

What if I forget to wash my hands, or I don't wash my hands thoroughly, and I touch my face and infect myself with the coronavirus? What if COVID-19 lives on groceries, and when I touch the packaging, I'm infected? What if I get sick and have to be hospitalized and can't afford my treatment? What if, when I'm in the hospital, no one can visit me, and I'm all alone in my struggle?

Does this mind-chatter sound familiar? It's completely normal to have concerns, worries, and anxieties during a pandemic of a highly transmissible, deadly virus. The threat is real, imminent, unpredictable, and invisible. The media incessantly covers apocalyptic scenes in COVID-19 hospital units with shortages of beds, lifesaving equipment, and personal protective equipment (PPE) for health-care workers, leading to unnecessary illness, disability, and death. These

127

stories and images haunt us as we shelter in place with little to distract us from the pandemic panic.

Given that there's no known cure or treatment yet, we do everything in our power to prevent the spread of the virus to ourselves and others. But, while knowing all the precautions to take against a deadly virus is important in keeping you healthy, our obsessive worrying over the virus—defined as perseverative cognition—can actually lower your immunity and make it more likely you will get sick.

Perseverative cognition is "the repeated or chronic activation of the cognitive representation of one or more psychological stressors." Worry and rumination involving stressful events, in the past or the future, are classified as perseverative cognition.

Most stressful events and our physiological responses to them are fleeting and, thus, unlikely to cause harm to our bodies and minds. But what happens when a stressful event is prolonged, with no end in sight? Prolonged physiological responses to continuous thoughts about stressors can weaken your system and increase the likelihood of trauma and disease.

Perseverative cognition can be likened to a dog chasing its tail. The more a dog tries unsuccessfully to catch his tail, the more determined and frustrated he becomes. It is a vicious cycle with no end. And when we're stuck in a cycle, we're more depressed, more likely to abuse alcohol, overeat, or take medication to take the edge off—to break the cycle and shut it all down. No wonder! We need a reprieve from ourselves. In particular, perseverative cognition can also trigger the stress response and put people at greater risk for cardiovascular disease. Thinking about stress, or rather obsessing over it, establishes a link between stress and disease. Worrying about anticipated events can raise cortisol levels and heart rates and increase wear and tear on the body.

Perseverative cognition may have its roots in evolutionary development. Humans have always faced grave dangers, and our ability to navigate these dangers has determined whether we live or die. Thus, identifying and assessing danger are critical survival skills. If hunter-gatherers didn't outsmart predators, like woolly mammoths, they ran the risk of becoming mincemeat and not getting the food they needed to survive. If early humans living in cold climates didn't store enough food, they would starve to death. And, for humans today, if we don't effectively mask, wash our hands, and socially distance, we could contract and die from COVID-19. The ability to plot and plan to minimize risks and dangers is the reason humans have survived.

But when plotting and planning turn into perseverative cognition, our stress response goes into overdrive, making it easy to catastrophize and spiral into overwhelming dread and panic. Doing this leaves us feeling drained, anxious, overwhelmed, and depressed.

The thing to remember is that the worried voice inside our heads has good intentions; it wants to keep us safe, healthy, and alive, but it can lead us astray. The style and nature of your inner voice has its roots in nature and nurture. The way you speak to yourself stems from your physiology and brain chemistry, as well as the way your parents and other role models spoke to you. Perhaps you had a critical parent, who judged you at every turn. You likely internalized your parent's commentary out of both habit and survival. This voice can keep you stuck in your anxieties and worries and not allow you to break free. It may prevent you from taking measured and important risks that move your life forward. In other words, sometimes you need to thank the voice for its concern and tell it to take a hike!

How do you know when your thought chatter has become problematic? One clue is when your thoughts often start with "what if." "What ifs" tend to be drama queens, portending catastrophe. For example: *What if I don't get the promotion? What if I ask someone out and they reject me? What if I do poorly on my test? What if I lose my job? What if I get sick?* You'll notice that "what ifs" trigger fear and tend to paralyze you into inaction. But risk-taking is an important part of reaching your goals and achieving your dreams. Few who achieved great things did so by staying in their comfort zones and avoiding risks.

Think about your greatest achievements. Were they preceded by anxiety, worry, and fear? You likely pushed through the fear to pursue your goals anyway. If you had let fear keep you confined to your comfort zone, would you have pushed your limits and reached new heights? Probably not.

Worry Insurance and the Psychology of Worry

When you board an airplane, you hand your fate over to the pilot, aircraft mechanics, air traffic control, and weather conditions. The truth is, you have no control over whether your flight will safely take off, fly, and land. Yet some who fly obsessively worry while flying. Does the anxiety and worry help the plane stay aloft? Of course not. But many worriers believe if they didn't worry, the plane might go down. This is called worry insurance. The worrier believes the act of worrying somehow lowers the likelihood of a dreaded outcome. They think if they stop worrying, they'll invite doom. In the case of the worried flier, anxiety accomplishes nothing but a stress response that the worrier has to manage, perhaps by drinking or popping pills.

The reality of life is that so many things are uncertain and outside of our control. We can't know for sure that we'll succeed in our jobs, find the love of our lives, and not get sick. It takes a leap of faith to live every day with optimism and hope when we know how little control we have over our lives.

What Actually Makes Us Happy?

In the modern world, it seems that happiness—the opposite of perseverative cognition—is the holy grail. There are millions of books, articles, TED Talks, YouTube videos, and workshops that promise to deliver this goal of well-being: happiness. Still, why does it feel so out of reach? Perhaps because we're chasing the wrong things. We've got our eyes on the glitzy, dazzling prizes of wealth, status, fame, and the perfect body, when none of these things has been shown to bring peace of mind and lasting happiness. We want and pursue things that keep us locked in a cycle of discontent. Seeking out materialism simply makes people less happy.

Richard Easterlin, a professor of economics at the University of Southern California, noticed a strange paradox involving money and happiness. If a positive correlation existed between the two, we would expect citizens of developed countries to be happier than those of developing nations. But overall, more prosperous countries are no happier than their poorer counterparts. These findings, known as the Easterlin Paradox, contradict popular assumptions that more affluent people have happier lives.

So, if all the stuff we've been led to believe doesn't make us happy, what does?

Happiness Quotient

Research has shown that the things that make us happy include living in the present, seeking fulfilling work, engaging in acts of kindness, practicing gratitude, meditating for mindfulness, and fostering a sense of connection. These things constitute our happiness quotient. In other words, mostly intrinsically satisfying pursuits—ones that make us feel like we're using our gifts in the world, appreciating what we have, making the world a better place, lifting people and ourselves up, and being an essential part of our communities. How can we learn to want the things that make us happy instead of the things we think make us happy?

What are some better ways of wanting?

Kickstarting Happiness

Now that we know what brings us happiness, how do we attain it? Does the act of knowing what brings happiness achieve it for us? Unfortunately, no. Happiness is an ever-changing state that ebbs and flows based on internal and external forces. Rather than being tossed about in a sea of emotions and reactions and going along for the ride, you can cultivate happiness through intentional practice. The good news is you have control over it. The bad news is it doesn't just happen; you must persevere until it becomes ingrained. Think of happiness as a habit, just like brushing your teeth or exercising. At first, it may seem like just one more chore to add to your lengthy to-do list, but once it becomes part of the fabric of your life, you will reap the rewards.

What are some approaches for kickstarting happiness?

Living in the Present

Training in mindful awareness is an important cornerstone in the treatment for chronic worrying. Mindfulness emphasizes focusing our mental energy on the present with openness and acceptance. When you worry, you're focused on the future or obsessing over the past, so focusing your attention on the *present* is a powerful way to reduce your worries and ruminations. You can get started by staying attuned to the here and now while doing simple things like cooking, taking a walk, gardening, or enjoying the company of a friend.

Going with Flow

You've heard the expression, *go with the flow*, which means to take things as they come. In the case of work, *going with flow* is the secret to happiness. Flow is a state of being fully immersed, energized, and enjoying what you're doing. Most of us must spend the better part of our lives working to earn a living, so it's best if you can seek jobs that allow you to use your strengths and lead to flourishing. There's research by Martin Seligman, director of the Penn Positive Psychology Center and Zellerbach Family Professor of Psychology in the Penn Department of Psychology. He's found that if, at work, you feel you're using signature strengths or character strengths most essential to who you are, it boosts happiness and reduces depression. Using your signature strengths increases your productivity and job satisfaction and thus happiness.

What makes a job a calling—one that gives us meaning? According to research by Mihaly Csikszentmihalyi, a Hungarian-American psychologist, jobs and activities that give us flow boost our happiness. When you're so engaged in activities you lose track of time, you're experiencing flow. To achieve flow, you must tackle projects and tasks that are reasonably challenging, ones for which you have the skills to meet the challenge.

In our leisure time, we often choose activities that are passive, such as scrolling through our social media feeds, surfing YouTube, or searching for shows on Netflix. Even though we think we prefer these things, people report being bored and apathetic while engaged in these activities. So, choosing hobbies that challenge you and during which you're creating, learning, or stretching yourself are better choices. Examples include learning a language, mastering a software program, creating a video, solving puzzles, participating in a game, or playing a musical instrument.

Practicing Gratitude

Taking a moment out of your day to give thanks for the good things in your life is a powerful way to kickstart happiness. Research shows that taking time each day to experience gratitude can boost happiness and health. Some people reading this might think, *there are many days when I have nothing to be thankful for.* When we think of gifts, we typically think of big things, like landing a lucrative job, receiving an unexpected financial windfall, or meeting your soulmate. But gratitude practice includes focusing on the small things as well—a beautiful spring day, food on the table, or a satisfying connection with a friend. In fact, it takes more practice to notice and appreciate the small things because we may take them for granted in our pursuit of the big things. But by appreciating only the big things, we are missing the other things that make for a rich and contented life.

An added happiness bonus is openly sharing gratitude for other people. If you're thankful for someone, tell them—in person, in writing, or through a gesture. Expressing gratitude for another can have positive ripple effects in your happiness quotient.

For the next week, take ten or fifteen minutes each day to write down five things you're grateful for. As you jot them down, linger over the things you're writing about. Picture the people, places, or things, and be mindful of your feelings of gratitude for each item you've written down.

Acts of Kindness

In our material world, many believe that the accumulation of cool things brings us happiness—having the latest and greatest gizmos with all the bells and whistles will give us a happiness boost. Those who buy themselves much-hyped toys are happier—right? Actually, no. In fact, a 2008 study gave participants the task of either giving away money or spending money on oneself. The results were surprising. They found that giving away money as opposed to spending money on oneself is more beneficial to mood and a sense of well-being.

Acts of kindness are things we do for others, expecting nothing in return. In our what's in it for me (WIIFM) culture, acts of kindness surprise and delight people because they're not used to getting something for nothing. Acts of kindness don't have to involve money or material things. They can be things such as:

- Making masks for the COVID-19 pandemic and giving them away for free.
- Stopping to chat with an elderly neighbor, even though you are in a hurry.

- Helping a coworker on a project, even though it will increase your workload.
- Offering to grocery shop for a disabled person in your community.
- Cooking a meal for a family who's facing hard times.

For the next week or two, give acts of kindness a try, and then tune into your level of happiness. Plan to do one or more acts of kindness each day. Observe your happiness quotient. Do you notice you are happier immediately after the act of kindness? Does it have ripple effects throughout the day or even the week? If it does, you may want to consider making this a permanent part of your life.

Meditating for Mindfulness

According to neuroscience, the default state of our brains is a wandering mind. In fact, 50 percent of the time, our thoughts are time-traveling backward or forward, not centered on the present (Killingsworth and Gilbert). This state of mind is also called "monkey-mind" in Eastern philosophies. This distracted state kicks in quickly whenever we're not focused on a given activity or task. When it takes over, you're thinking outside the here and now, reviewing past events or looking toward the future. While this is a superpower unique to humans, research has found that mind-wandering has a negative impact on happiness. Why? Because we're distracted from the present moment.

Why is focusing on the present so important? First of all, because if you're not, you're missing out on life as it happens. You're in a past state, likely critiquing yourself, or in a future state that hasn't yet happened. And unless you're a fortune teller, you have no way of knowing what's coming. Trying to control uncertain future events tends to cause anxiety because it's an impossible task. Similarly, trying to change the past is a waste of precious time.

Our untrained minds are a bit like a new puppy. If we let our new puppy behave according to his adorable puppy instincts, he pees in the house, shreds anything he gets his paws on, barks uncontrollably, and jumps up on people. As we train the puppy, he learns the behaviors that make him a well-behaved, loyal, and playful companion.

How can we stop our minds from jumping around and taking us for a wild ride? By turning our minds away from distracting thoughts toward a single focus point, thus turning off the default network. Meditation can make us happier because it stops mind-wandering. It also has benefits like building brain tissue and strengthening your brain over time. How frequently should you do it to achieve these benefits? Meditate for thirty minutes every day. If you find that this is too long in the beginning, start with twenty minutes and increase the duration over time.

Fostering a Sense of Connection

A sense of belonging and connection is a huge part of the happiness quotient. In this context, connection is defined as face-to-face human contact that forms the fabric of social relationships. It's knowing others and being known. It's one smile, one hello, one kind gesture at a time. It's chatting with your barista about his divorce. It's telling your neighbor you're sorry she lost her job. It's sharing a laugh with a guy in the line at the pharmacy. You build community brick by brick, until you have a place where you feel you belong, a place that fulfills your social needs.

We have high-tech devices that are miraculous in many ways, but the way we use them interferes with our need for social engagement. If we use them to distance or disengage from others, they erode our social fabric and tear down our communities, one social connection at a time. Imagine you have the opportunity to chat with someone sitting next to you in a café, but instead, you whip out your digital device. The other person, in turn, does the same. You may be interacting with others digitally, but you've missed the opportunity right in front of you to engage and put another brick in the wall of your community, your place of belonging. This estranges you from the person next to you, further limiting your social connections.

Many people don't understand the importance of social connection for well-being. The quality and quantity of individuals' social relationships has been linked not only to mental health but also to both morbidity and mortality. Research indicates that a lack of social connection is a greater detriment to health than obesity, smoking, and high blood pressure. Social connection strengthens our immune system, helps us recover from disease faster, and may even lengthen our life. People who feel more connected have lower rates of anxiety and depression.

To be human is to have the ability to reflect on the past and project into the future. These cognitive gifts have enabled humans to learn from history, make remarkable progress, and create architectural, artistic, technological, and other masterpieces. The downside of these cognitive abilities is perseverative cognition or excessive worry, which can paralyze us and keep happiness at arm's length.

Further, what we've been taught to believe will make us happy doesn't, so we must re-orient ourselves to want what does. It turns out that intrinsically satisfying pursuits are the holy grail of happiness. Once we've met our basic needs, constantly reaching for material things is a fool's game in that those things will never give us the satisfaction of living in the present, doing fulfilling work, engaging in acts of kindness, practicing gratitude, meditating for mindfulness, and fostering a sense of connection.

CHAPTER 14

BECOMING SOCIALLY AWARE

People Who Need People

We've never had such a vast array of technology tools at our fingertips to communicate with each other—texting, video phone calling, video conferencing, Snapchatting, tweeting, Facebooking, instant messaging—and yet loneliness is an epidemic in America. With all this so-called connecting, what's going on? Are the tools making us lonelier? Isolated people look to the digital world in vain to allay their feelings of seclusion. Using tech tools to connect with others can make you feel you have less need for face-to-face social interactions. Research shows that loneliness is caused by a lack of depth in relationships, a lack of true intimacy. In other words, you believe they scratch the itch, but the itch remains.

With the coronavirus pandemic dramatically transforming our society overnight, the in-person, social nature of our world has been scaled way back, and social distancing—masks and all—has amplified loneliness. By necessity, we've been relegated to collaborative technology tools and social media to squeeze intimacy out of our digital devices. It's the best we can do now, especially when lives and health are at stake. But the reality is that people need people—to look in their eyes, bask in their smiles, feel their hugs, relish in the comfort of touch, and enjoy each other's presence. To feel less alone in this vast universe, on our blue-green planet spinning around the sun. To remember we belong to each other.

Managing Digital Distractions

We've all had the experience of being fully present in the moment—perhaps enjoying time with a friend—when we checked our smartphone, got jerked out of the moment and yanked down a rabbit hole. We couldn't resist the allure of the device in our hands.

In many ways, we are fortunate to live in an age with a world of information at our fingertips and with digital devices that give us access to that world. Given that digital distraction is available 24-7, we must make sure our digital tools enhance rather than detract from our quality of life. If we mindlessly get pulled into the universe of posting, commenting, liking, tweeting, messaging, Instagramming, and YouTubing, we'll have lost the battle.

We can manage digital distraction by turning our devices off, going dark, and hiding the apps or social media programs that pull us in with their familiar icons that promise an inviting multimedia scrolling experience. Turn off push notifications, silence texts, and cut the digital umbilical cord—at some point every day, if possible. If we pace ourselves, mindfully engage, and keep our distractions at a minimum, we'll control our digital devices and not the other way around.

Living for Likes

If you live for likes or positive strokes from folks, what happens when you don't get the responses you were hoping for? Your mood craters, and then you're stuck with a mood problem. With unchecked social media use, your happiness and well-being are on a roller-coaster ride of external approval. Crowdsourcing your happiness is hazardous.

If you think social media is trashing your life, or even limiting its potential, you may want to consider a social media fast. A fast allows you to rediscover yourself without peering through the distorted prism of likes and follows, to live from the inside-out rather than the outside-in. It silences the external noise and allows you to hear the music of your internal voice, the melody that will have you dancing down a path of happiness.

Vetting News and Information in the Digital Age

In this era of fake news, hoaxes, and scams, the ability to discern the truth is critical. Within the minefield of fabricated news, information, and profiles, we need to cultivate the ability to seek truth to make the best possible decisions. It takes focus and drive to search for truth in the world, not simply consuming facts as they are packaged and fed to us. Content that's presented to the public often comes with a well-honed agenda to influence our thinking and behavior, whether to persuade you to purchase a given product, act in a certain way, or adopt a given political point of view. The more we seek the truth by vetting news and information, the better off we'll be. These strategies will help you separate fact from fiction:

- Identify news sources that are reliable, fair, and well-researched by checking their credentials.
- Ask: are multiple sources reporting a story? If only one source is reporting a story, it's probably fake news.
- Assess a publisher's credibility by checking its publication history.

- Look to see if the author of a given piece is real and credible.
- Check Wikipedia to see that sources and citations are legitimate.
- Tap fact-checking websites, such as Snopes.com, Factcheck. org, and TruthOrFiction.com.

Steering Clear of Victimhood

We all know people who are victim-y—everything that happens to them is someone else's fault. They never take responsibility for their circumstances. They live in a world of hard knocks where everyone is plotting against them in a giant conspiratorial web.

Victimhood—or the poor-me syndrome—is tempting because it keeps you safe from risk and blames others for your mistakes and shortcomings. People who fear failure may play the victim so they don't have to venture out and face their greatest fears. But playing the victim comes at a great cost. People who do this squander their time and potential and often end up bitter, disillusioned, and filled with regret.

Resist victimhood and instead pursue a life of strength, courage, and fulfillment. The good news is that you can prevent a victim mentality by:

- Recognizing what makes you feel powerless.
- Resisting the temptation to blame other people, groups, and institutions.
- Taking charge of your needs and desires.
- Taking responsibility for the circumstances in your life.
- Choosing your thoughts and feelings. You can't choose everything that happens to you, but you can choose your thoughts and feelings in response to those things.

Having Worthy Conversations

Think back on a conversation you had with a family member, friend, or colleague that left you inspired, invigorated, and ready to take action based on the ideas you shared. Perhaps you felt super-charged and motivated for days and got busy making things happen in your life.

Unfortunately, these exchanges are not as common as we'd like because conversations can fall prey to conversation-blockers, such as when they get preachy, victim-y, or blaming.

How can you consistently have worthier conversations? By remaining open, generative, inspired, and action oriented. Come to the conversation without preconceived notions. Allow your conversation partner's words to open your eyes to new ways of doing and being. Explore ideas and solutions without judgment. Allow yourself to be inspired by the dialogue and learn something new by remaining open to the magic in the synergy of ideas and emotions. Conversations worth having change hearts and minds and inspire people to bring the ideas to life.

Doing What You Love without Going Crazy or Broke

When it comes to work and a career, how do you know what you'll love? Pick a career path that allows you to use the maximum amount of your innate gifts and talents. Then design your life around what you're good at *and* your need to earn a living. Let's say you love gaming, creating YouTube videos, and writing a novel; however, none of these are lucrative pursuits but rather hobbies. You decide to take a job as an instructional designer for a Fortune 500 company in which you create online courses, incorporating gaming for instruction, video creation, and scriptwriting. Is this your ideal life's work? No, but it pays you well to tap into your interests and gifts. Thus, you won't go broke or crazy from boredom. It's work that feeds your body and your soul.

Going for Work-Life Balance

As the old saying goes: all work and no play makes Jack a dull boy. But all play and no work makes Jack a party boy. Both lead to dissatisfaction and a sense that life is out of balance. To avoid either extreme, aim for work-life balance, which means choosing a profession or work that gives you the flexibility and time to pursue the things that bring meaning to your life. If you find work you love that brings meaning, you're one of the lucky ones. This isn't always possible; often, work is just a means to an end, which is why it's best to build time into your weekly schedule for things that make life worth living, such as your passions, pursuits, and loved ones. With enough of those tucked into your week, you won't feel that life is passing you by. If your focus is on balance, incorporating work and play, and you design your life accordingly, you are more likely to end the day with a smile.

Maximizing Financial Well-Being

Financial literacy isn't always taught in school, which is crazy because what's more important than having enough money to survive, or even better, to thrive? Given that it's essential to our well-being, we must teach ourselves financial literacy, including managing income flow, controlling expenses, saving, and investing. The earlier, the better. Not managing money well and living on the edge financially often fills us with anxiety, uncertainty, and dread, leading to other problems, such as substance abuse, which can, in turn, exacerbate financial problems. It becomes an impossible-to-break vicious cycle.

If you don't create a plan, you'll be a victim of your circumstances, and it could be a rough-and-tumble ride. The plan is summarized in a simple equation:

Generating Income + Wise Spending + Saving + Investing = Financial Well-Being

Have a plan in which you earn money doing something you like, spend wisely, and save and invest. Get comfortable with your financial situation—one that sets you up for a life well-lived, an essential part of the happiness equation.

Stepping Away from Your Emotions

Emotions—whether positive or negative—can be overpowering and cause us to lose ourselves. When emotions blindside us, detaching from them can be nearly impossible. But this is the very time we need to step back, gain perspective, and not let our emotions get the best of us. Why? Because they can propel us to do things we might regret. Like a dense fog, our feelings move in and blind us. When driving in the fog, you must shine your lights for maximum visibility and proceed with caution until the fog lifts. When our strong emotions have subsided, we can more clearly see the right action.

You are a vessel with a mind and heart through which energy moves. Energy shows up in the form of thoughts in your mind and emotions in your heart. Remember: you have thoughts, but you are not your thoughts. Similarly, you have emotions, but you are not your emotions. Let it flow. Let it go.

Cultivating Conscious Living

Consciousness, the state of being awake and in touch with one's thoughts, emotions, and actions, helps you become more aware of how you move through the world and the way you react to people and experiences.

Cultivating consciousness without chemical enhancement may be the best, cheapest high around. To get there, though, you must face reality head-on, which can be invigorating and terrifying and everything in between. Start cultivating consciousness immediately through meditation, journaling, practicing introspection, listening more, pursuing lifelong learning, and wandering and wondering. Try all these recommendations or just sample a few, and you'll be on the path to conscious living.

Understanding the Rhythm of Life: Love and Loss

It can be said that love and loss are two parts of the whole of life. Rarely, if ever, do you have love without loss. Does that mean you should approach love fixated on the fact that you will likely lose that love one day? Absolutely not. You will hold back and not give love everything you've got. Your apprehension will diminish your experience of love. Simply trust that you can survive the loss of a love when it happens. Know the gaping hole that remains will be painful for a time but will fill up with another love, another passion, another sense of purpose. Love and loss are the rhythm of life—the filling up and emptying of your heart.

The minute we're born, we face an eventual, inevitable loss—our own death. Even as we go forth into the world and strive to become the person we know we can be, we're aware that death awaits us. This fact doesn't stop most of us from fully living. In fact, this inevitable date with fate may motivate us to live each day as though it were our last and infuse meaning into our daily existence.

One cannot know happiness without knowing sadness. One cannot know light without darkness. Similarly, one cannot know love without loss. Accepting these opposites as the way of the world frees us to live without hesitation, to live with abandon.

The Psychology of Happiness

When asked what makes us happy, Americans tend to mention material things, such as money, a good job, a nice house and car, and fabulous vacations. And when we say, "good job," we usually mean one that's lucrative. This is how we've been conditioned in the U.S. We often measure things by financial and material success. While it's true that we need money to meet our basic needs of food, housing, and health care, the research simply doesn't show that our happiness primarily lies in material things. Long-lasting happiness comes from things that bring intrinsic satisfaction—that feed our hearts and minds, including meaningful work, acts of kindness, gratitude, meditating, and a sense of connection with one's community.

Uncertain times, such as living through a pandemic or an economic crisis, help us focus on what matters most. The superfluous parts of our lives fall away. We yearn to connect with the people who mean the most to us. We're motivated to help others in meaningful ways, for example, by handcrafting masks, donating to food banks, or volunteering to Zoom with an elderly person on lockdown in a senior living facility. We nurture ourselves in ways we didn't when life moved at a breakneck speed—making time for reflection and meditation, preparing healthy home-cooked meals, and taking walks while noticing the world around us instead of staring at our phones.

For many of us a crisis, like a pandemic, forces us to press pause and ask the question, *Have I been living the life I want?* And if our answer is "no," we must seize the moment to change our lives so that we're smiling at the end of each day.

Source Links

Chapter 1: The Great Shift in the Human Condition

https://www.cigna.com/newsroom/news-releases/2018/
new-cigna-study-reveals-loneliness-at-epidemic-levels-in-america

https://www.forbes.com/sites/neilhowe/2019/05/03/
millennials-and-the-loneliness-epidemic/#4c6729617676

https://psychcentral.com/blog/
understanding-the-loneliness-epidemic/

https://www.psychologytoday.com/us/blog/modern-mentali-
ty/201807/what-you-need-know-about-the-loneliness-epidemic

https://www.hrsa.gov/enews/past-issues/2019/january-17/
loneliness-epidemic

https://www.cigna.com/newsroom/news-releases/2018/
new-cigna-study-reveals-loneliness-at-epidemic-levels-in-america

https://www.psychologytoday.com/us/blog/
modern-mentality/201807/what-you-need-know-about-the-loneli-
ness-epidemic

https://www.forbes.com/sites/laurashin/2014/11/14/10-steps-to-
conquering-information-overload/#5dea453a7b08

https://www.thedailybeast.com/in-praise-of-doing-nothing

https://www.inc.com/erik-sherman/workers-are-allergic-to-robots-
ai-says-new-research.html

Chapter 2: Social Media: The Great Social Experiment

https://www.nielsen.com/us/en/insights/article/2018/time-flies-us-
adults-now-spend-nearly-half-a-day-interacting-with-media/

https://www.socialmediatoday.com/marketing/
how-much-time-do-people-spend-social-media-infographic

https://www.huffpost.com/entry/how-much-time-on-social-media_
n_5be9c148e4b0783e0a1a8281

Chapter 3: Victimhood as Currency

https://quillette.com/2018/05/17/understanding-victimhood-cul-
ture-interview-bradley-campbell-jason-manning/

https://www.theatlantic.com/politics/archive/2015/09/
the-problems-with-the-term-victimhood-culture/406057/

https://www.researchgate.net/
publication/272408166_Microaggression_and_Moral_Cultures

https://www.theepochtimes.com/the-costs-and-benefits-of-victim-
hood_3031699.html

https://www.gotoquiz.com/victim_or_victor_what_s_your_mindset

Chapter 5: Preventing Digital Distractions

https://www.forbes.com/sites/bernardmarr/2018/05/21/how-much-
data-do-we-create-every-day-the-mind-blowing-stats-everyone-
should-read/#163cd61c60ba

https://www.fastcompany.com/3051417/
why-its-so-hard-to-pay-attention-explained-by-science

https://virtual-addiction.com/digital-distraction-test/

https://curiosity.com/topics/you-can-build-deep-work-skills-to-in-
crease-productivity-curiosity/

https://goskybound.com/tips-for-curbing-digital-distractions/

Chapter 6: Truth-Seeking: The New IQ Measure in the Digital Age

https://www.forbes.com/sites/trevornace/2018/04/04/
only-two-thirds-of-american-millennials-believe-the-earth-is-
round/#239b49607ec6

https://factsandtrends.net/2018/08/07/
ways-to-communicate-truth-in-a-fake-news-era/

https://www.techspot.com/news/78029-over-40-percent-activity-
internet-fake.html

https://lifehacker.com/how-to-outsmart-algorithms-and-take-con-
trol-of-your-inf-1834893542

Chapter 8: Doing What You Love Doesn't Have to Leave You Broke or Drive You Crazy

https://www.indeed.com/career-advice/finding-a-job/
how-to-choose-a-career

https://blog.rescuetime.com/time-blocking-101/

https://www.theatlantic.com/health/archive/2019/05/
work-life-balance/590662/

Chapter 11: Consciousness is the Ultimate Drug

https://americanaddictioncenters.org/rehab-guide/
addiction-statistics

https://brainworksneurotherapy.com/what-are-brainwaves

https://eocinstitute.org/meditation/
meditation-for-the-mind-how-meditation-affects-consciousness/

https://ideas.ted.com/the-right-way-to-be-introspective-yes-theres-
a-wrong-way/

https://hbr.org/2012/05/make-your-enemies-your-allies

Chapter 13: The Psychology of Happiness

https://www.researchgate.net/publication/301311827_My_
Better_Self_Using_Strengths_at_Work_and_Work_Productivity_
Organizational_Citizenship_Behavior_and_Satisfaction

https://www.psychologytoday.com/us/blog/feeling-it/201208/
connect-thrive